THE COMPLETE SOCIAL SECURITY BIBLE

A PRACTICAL GUIDE TO CLAIMING STRATEGIES, BENEFITS, TAXES & MEDICARE TO AVOID COSTLY MISTAKES, INCREASE RETIREMENT INCOME & PLAN WITH CONFIDENCE

ADAM HENDERSON

CONTENTS

❀ Formatted with Vellum

INTRODUCTION: YOUR ROADMAP TO CONFIDENT RETIREMENT DECISIONS

Why These Decisions Matter More Than Ever

A single Social Security filing decision, made on a single afternoon, can change your monthly income for the rest of your life. For some people, that difference is hundreds of dollars every month. Over a twenty or thirty-year retirement, the gap between a well-timed claim and a poorly timed one can add up to tens of thousands of dollars, and sometimes more than $100,000 in lifetime benefits.

That number sounds dramatic, but it is real. Many Americans claim their benefits before reaching Full Retirement Age (FRA), which is the age at which you qualify for 100% of your calculated benefit. Many of those early filers do so without fully understanding the permanent reduction they lock in. Others miss spousal strategies, survivor planning opportunities, or Medicare enrollment windows that can trigger penalties you cannot simply undo later.

The rules governing Social Security and Medicare are genuinely complex. The Social Security Administration's policy guidance spans thousands of pages, and the details matter. Congress has layered decades of amendments, exceptions, and special provisions on top of the original program. The tough part is that the decisions you face are often permanent, or at least hard to reverse. You can change your car, your investment portfolio, even your career. But once you have been receiving Social Security benefits for more than twelve months, your claiming age is essentially set.

Here is the encouraging part: you do not need to become an expert on every rule. You need to understand the rules that apply to your situation, know what questions to ask, spot the expensive mistakes before you make them, and feel steady enough to act. That is what this book is built to help you do.

Whether you are sixty-two and wondering if early claiming makes sense, sixty-six and trying to coordinate benefits with a spouse, or seventy and already collecting but worried about taxes and Medicare premiums, the pages ahead focus on the decisions still in front of you.

How to Use This Book Effectively

Every chapter follows a consistent structure, so you know what you are getting. Each one opens with the core concept in plain language, then moves into real-life scenarios that show how the rules play out. Along the way, you will see common mistakes called out through clearly marked Mistake Alerts, and each chapter ends with action steps you can take right away.

You will also find tables, worksheets, and visual references throughout the book where you can compare options at a glance, record your own numbers, and track deadlines.

The checklist-driven approach matters because retirement benefit decisions have a lot of moving parts. Your Social Security claiming age, your spouse's age and work history, your Medicare enrollment window, your taxable income in retirement, and your health all interact. Checklists help you avoid skipping a critical step when the stakes are high and the rules are unforgiving.

Here is how to decide whether to read straight through or jump to specific chapters. If you are more than five years from filing, read the guide from start to finish. The early chapters build the foundation that makes the later strategy chapters make sense. If you are within a year or two of filing, or you already receive benefits, start with the chapter that matches your most pressing question. Then circle back to the chapters on taxes, Medicare, and the before-you-file checklist. Every chapter defines its own terms, so you will not be lost if you skip ahead.

The final chapters are designed as reference tools. The glossary defines every acronym and technical term in one place. The current-year numbers guide gives you a single spot to verify thresholds, limits, and deadlines that change annually. You can come back to these sections year after year as your situation changes.

What Makes This Guide Different

Most retirement guides fall into one of two traps. They either bury you in technical jargon lifted straight from government publications, or they simplify the rules so much that the advice turns generic and unreliable. This guide does not do either.

Every explanation here starts in plain English. When a technical term appears, such as Primary Insurance Amount (PIA) or Income-Related Monthly Adjustment Amount (IRMAA), it is defined immediately and tied to what it means for your monthly check or your Medicare premium. You will not be asked to memorize acronyms. You will understand what they mean and why they matter to you.

This guide also puts real weight on current-year verification. Social Security thresholds, Medicare premiums, tax brackets, and annual earnings limits change every year. Rather than relying on numbers that may be outdated by the time you read this, the text prompts you to confirm key figures through SSA.gov, Medicare.gov, or IRS.gov before you make a decision based on a specific dollar amount. If you are going to act on a number, it should be the right one.

You will also see scenarios drawn from a wide range of retirement situations. You will meet married couples weighing whether to stagger their claims, a divorced woman learning she qualifies for benefits on an ex-spouse's record, a widower choosing between his own retirement benefit and a survivor benefit, a self-employed consultant whose uneven income history affects her calculation, and an adult daughter helping her father make sense of a Medicare penalty notice. These are the kinds of decisions people actually face. The point is not theory. It is seeing how a rule lands when the details look a lot like yours.

Your Decision-Making Framework

Before you read another page, get clear on where you stand right now. Your situation determines which chapters matter most and which decisions are urgent. Three factors sit under every solid retirement benefit decision: your circumstances, your timeline, and whether you need professional help.

Start with a personal situation assessment. Are you single, married, divorced, or widowed? Are you still working, planning to work part-time, or fully retired? Do you have a pension from a government job? Is your health strong, uncertain, or are you managing a serious condition? Each of these details changes which Social Security and Medicare strategies apply. As you read, keep your own answers in view. The chapters ahead show how each factor can change your options.

Next is your timeline. If you are five years away from turning sixty-two, you have time to plan on purpose, check your earnings record for errors, estimate different claiming scenarios, and coordinate with a spouse. If you are three months away from turning sixty-five, Medicare deadlines stop being background noise and start being a real problem. Knowing your timeline tells you what needs attention now and what can wait.

Then look for signs you may want professional guidance. If your situation involves a government pension, a complex divorce, significant investment income, a business sale, or a seriously ill spouse, the way Social Security rules, tax law, and Medicare provisions interact can be hard to untangle on your own. A fee-only financial advisor or a certified Social Security claiming specialist can help you model scenarios and avoid expensive oversights. Throughout this guide, you will see clear indicators for when a situation is complicated enough that outside input may save you money, time, or a mistake that is hard to reverse.

Keep your circumstances, your timeline, and your support needs in mind as you move forward. The chapters ahead walk through how your benefit is calculated, the major claiming decisions, and the tax and Medicare issues that catch people off guard. Start with the chapter that fits your next decision.

1

HOW SOCIAL SECURITY REALLY CALCULATES YOUR BENEFITS

Every month, the Social Security Administration (SSA) sends payments to more than 70 million Americans. The amount isn't the same for everyone. It comes from a formula that pulls from decades of your working life. If you understand how the formula works, you can spot mistakes on your record, estimate your future benefit with more accuracy, and make clearer decisions about when to stop working or when to file.

In this chapter, we'll walk through the calculation from start to finish. You'll learn which years of earnings count, how the SSA turns those earnings into a monthly benefit, how to read your Social Security statement, and what to do if something on your record doesn't look right.

The 35-Year Earnings Rule Explained

Your Social Security benefit is based on your highest 35 years of earnings. The SSA reviews every year you paid Social Security taxes, from your first job through your most recent tax return. Then it picks the 35 years in which you earned the most, adjusted for inflation. Those 35 years become the base for your monthly benefit.

If you worked exactly 35 years, the math is simple: the SSA uses all of them. If you worked more than 35 years, only the highest-earning 35 count. Lower-earning years from early in your career, part-time work in college, or a period when you took a pay cut to switch fields may drop out of the calculation, replaced by stronger years.

Trouble shows up when you have fewer than 35 years of earnings. The SSA still plugs 35 numbers into the formula. For any year you did not work or did not earn enough to get credit, a zero goes into the calculation. Every zero drags your average down.

Think about it this way. Say you worked 30 solid years and earned a good income. Those five missing years each contribute a zero. Averaging five zeros in with 30 real earning years can cut your monthly benefit by a meaningful amount, potentially $100 to $200 per month or more, depending on your history.

That's why late-career earnings can matter so much. If you are 60 and weighing whether to keep working a little longer, those extra years of income can replace zeros or low-earning years from decades ago. Each added year can bump a weaker year out of the top 35 and strengthen your average. The SSA updates your earnings record and may recalculate your benefit when new wage data are received, but this does not always result in an immediate or annual increase in your monthly payment. That means improvements can show up even after you start collecting, but not necessarily right away.

How the 35-Year Rule Works

Social Security uses your highest 35 years of inflation-adjusted earnings.
If you have fewer than 35 years of earnings, zeros are included in the average.

Scenario	Earnings Included in the 35-Year Calculation	Total Earnings Used	Average Indexed Monthly Earnings (AIME)
1 **Worked 35 full years**	35 years at an average of $60,000	$2,100,000	$5,000/month
2 **Worked only 30 years**	30 years at $60,000 + 5 years at $0	$1,800,000	$4,286/month
3 **Worked 5 more years and replaced the zeros**	35 years at an average of $60,000	$2,100,000	$5,000/month

What This Means

- Fewer than 35 years of earnings means zeros lower your average.
- Additional working years can replace zero or low-earning years.
- A higher earnings average can increase your future benefit.

Simplified example for illustration only. Actual Social Security calculations also use wage indexing, bend points, and claiming age rules.

How Your Primary Insurance Amount Is Determined

After the SSA identifies your highest 35 years of earnings, it converts those earnings into one monthly number: your Primary Insurance Amount (PIA). Your PIA is the benefit you would receive if you claim at your Full Retirement Age (FRA). Calculations for early claiming, delayed retirement credits, and several family benefit rules all start here.

It happens in two steps.

Step one: calculating your Average Indexed Monthly Earnings (AIME). AIME is calculated by dividing the sum of inflation-adjusted earnings by 420 months (which is 35 years multiplied by 12 months). The result is your AIME, a single monthly dollar amount that represents your average inflation-adjusted earnings across your best working years.

Put simply, AIME is your average monthly earnings across your strongest 35 years, converted into today's dollars.

Step two: applying the benefit formula with bend points. The SSA does not give you a flat percentage of your AIME. Instead, it uses a progressive formula that replaces a higher share of income for lower earners and a smaller share for higher earners. The Social Security benefit formula uses two bend points that change annually with inflation.

For someone reaching age 62, the formula works like this (bend points are examples; verify current-year amounts at SSA.gov):

- The benefit formula replaces 90% of the first portion of AIME up to the first bend point.
- The benefit formula replaces 32% of AIME between the first and second bend points.
- The benefit formula replaces 15% of AIME above the second bend point.

Add those three amounts together, and you have your PIA.

Here's what that means for your check. The formula is built so that lower-income workers replace a larger share of their pre-retirement earnings through Social Security, while higher-income workers replace a smaller share. Someone who averaged $30,000 per year over their career may see Social Security replace roughly 50 to 60 % of that income. Someone who averaged $150,000 may see closer to 25 to 30 % replaced.

Cost-of-Living Adjustments (COLAs) also affect your PIA over time. Each year, if the Consumer Price Index rises, the SSA increases benefits to keep pace with inflation. These adjustments begin applying to your PIA starting at age 62, even if you have not claimed it yet. By the time you file, your benefit reflects the COLAs that occurred in the meantime.

Understanding Your Social Security Statement

Your Social Security statement is one of the most useful documents you can pull for retirement planning. It shows your year-by-year earnings history, estimates your future monthly benefit at different claiming ages, and gives you a chance to catch mistakes before they follow you into retirement.

You can access your statement online by creating a my Social Security account at SSA.gov. If you are 60 or older and do not have an online account, the SSA mails a paper statement about three months before your birthday each year.

Reading your earnings history. Start with the year-by-year record of your taxed earnings. Each line shows the year and the wages reported to the SSA by your employers (or, if you are self-employed, the net earnings you reported on your tax return). This is the data the SSA uses for your benefit calculation.

Go through this list slowly. Compare it to your own records, such as old tax returns or W-2 forms. Watch for years that show zero when you know you worked. Pay attention to amounts that look low compared to what you remember. If you held multiple jobs in one year, make sure all income appears.

Projected benefit estimates. Your statement shows estimated monthly benefits at three ages: 62, your Full Retirement Age, and 70. These estimates assume you will keep earning at roughly your current level until the claiming age shown. If you expect to stop working earlier, cut back, or shift into lower-paying work, the estimates may come in higher than what you'll actually receive.

The SSA updates these estimates each year using your most recent earnings. If you had a low-income year or stopped working, you may see the projections drop a bit the following year.

When estimates might be wrong. Your statement estimates are projections, not guarantees. They can be off for several reasons:

- They assume you keep working at your current income level until the age shown
- They do not account for prior reductions under the Windfall Elimination Provision (WEP) or Government Pension Offset (GPO), which were repealed by the Social Security Fairness Act, effective January 2024
- They cannot predict future COLA increases
- If your earnings record contains errors, the estimates are based on incorrect data

If you want a more precise projection as you get closer to retirement, use the SSA's online calculators, especially the Detailed Calculator at SSA.gov. You can also call and request a benefits estimate based on your actual record.

Check Your Social Security Earnings Record

Use this worksheet to compare your own records with your Social Security statement and note any discrepancies that may need follow-up.

Before You Start

- Log in to your my Social Security account.
- Download or print your earnings history.
- Gather old W-2s or tax returns if available.

Year	Your Record (W-2 / Tax Return)	SSA Statement Amount	Match?	Notes / Discrepancy
			☐ Yes ☐ No	
			☐ Yes ☐ No	
			☐ Yes ☐ No	
			☐ Yes ☐ No	
			☐ Yes ☐ No	
			☐ Yes ☐ No	
			☐ Yes ☐ No	
			☐ Yes ☐ No	
			☐ Yes ☐ No	
			☐ Yes ☐ No	
			☐ Yes ☐ No	

What to Watch For

- A year showing $0 when you know you worked
- Income that looks lower than expected
- Missing earnings after a name change
- Any year that does not match your records

Next Steps

Years I need to investigate: ____________________

Documents I need to gather: ____________________

SSA follow-up date: ____________________

***Tip:** If you need more space, copy this worksheet and continue on another page.*

Common Errors and How to Fix Them

Errors on Social Security records are more common than most people expect. The SSA processes hundreds of millions of wage reports each year, and mistakes happen. If they go uncorrected, they can reduce your monthly benefit for life.

Missing years on your record. Sometimes entire years disappear. That can happen if an employer filed paperwork under a slightly different version of your name, if a small business failed to report wages correctly, or if records were lost during a system change. A missing year becomes a zero in your 35-year calculation. Even one missing year of solid earnings can lower your PIA.

Incorrect wage reporting. You might see a year where the amount is lower than what you earned. This can happen when an employer reports wages incorrectly, when only part of your income shows up because of a mid-year job change, or when self-employment income was underreported on your tax return. If you earned $52,000 in a year but only $38,000 appears on your record, that gap affects your average.

Name change documentation issues. If you changed your name because of marriage, divorce, or another reason and didn't update your records with the SSA, earnings under your previous name may not have been linked correctly to your account. This is a common cause of missing earnings, particularly for women who changed their name early in their career and never notified the SSA at the time.

How to request a correction. If you find an error, contact the SSA with documentation. Useful evidence includes W-2 forms, pay stubs, tax returns, or a letter from a former employer confirming wages. The SSA has a formal process to correct earnings records. Catching and fixing an error sooner is usually easier. Records older than three years can still be corrected, but the paper trail is often harder to pull together.

You can call the SSA at 1-800-772-1213, visit a local office, or start the correction process through your online account. Keep copies of anything you submit.

Mistake Alert and Real-Life Scenario

Mistake Alert: Skipping a review of your Social Security earnings record before you claim can cost you real money. When you file, the SSA calculates your PIA using whatever is on your record at that moment. If an error has been sitting there for 20 years, it gets built into the benefit. Fixing it after you claim is possible, but it can take longer, involve more back-and-forth, and require documents you may not have anymore.

Real-Life Scenario: Maria Discovers a Missing Year

Maria is 63 and plans to claim Social Security at her Full Retirement Age of 67. She creates a my Social Security account and checks her earnings history for the first time. On the year-by-year list, she sees that 2004 shows zero earnings. She knows she worked full-time that year at a small accounting firm.

Maria digs through her files and finds her 2004 W-2 showing $47,500 in wages. She also finds her tax return from that year, confirming the income was reported to the IRS. With that documentation, she contacts the SSA.

After she submits her evidence, the SSA investigates and confirms that the employer failed to report her wages correctly that year. Her record is corrected, and the $47,500 is added back to her earnings history.

How this error compounded over time. With the zero in place, Maria's 35-year average included one blank year, which pulled down her AIME. Once corrected, her AIME increased, which raised her PIA. For Maria, the difference was about $38 per month. Over a 20-year retirement, that one correction adds up to more than $9,000 in benefits.

If Maria had waited until after filing to check her record, or never checked at all, she would have collected a lower benefit for the rest of her life without knowing what caused the shortfall.

Steps to correct your record:

1. Log in to your my Social Security account at SSA.gov
2. Review your earnings history year by year
3. Compare each year to your own records (tax returns, W-2s, pay stubs)
4. Note any years that show zero or a lower amount than expected
5. Gather supporting documentation for any discrepancies
6. Contact the SSA by phone, online, or in person to request a correction
7. Follow up until you receive confirmation that the change has been made

Chapter Checklist and Verification Tips

Use this checklist to confirm your Social Security earnings record is accurate and that your benefit estimate is based on the right inputs. Ideally, do this before you file, while old records are still accessible.

- Create or log in to your my Social Security account at SSA.gov
- Print or download your full earnings history
- Compare each year of listed earnings against your tax returns or W-2 forms
- Flag any year showing zero earnings when you know you worked
- Flag any year showing lower earnings than you recall
- Check that your name on file matches the name used on all past employer records

- If you changed your name at any point, confirm that the SSA linked all earnings under both names
- Note whether you have at least 35 years of earnings (fewer than 35 means zeros are in your calculation)
- If you are still working, estimate how additional years may improve your benefit by replacing weaker years
- If you find errors, gather documentation and contact the SSA promptly
- Verify that your projected benefit estimates on the statement reflect your actual work plans going forward
- Check SSA.gov for current-year bend points and COLA adjustments to understand how your PIA may change

Verification tips:

Check your earnings record at least once per year, especially if you changed jobs, became self-employed, or had a year with unusual income. The SSA has a limited window in which corrections are typically easier to process using standard documentation. After three years, corrections are still possible, but you may need more supporting proof.

If your statement shows an estimate that seems lower than expected, the reason is usually one of three issues: fewer than 35 years of earnings, one or more errors in the earnings record, or an assumption you will keep earning at your current level when you actually plan to stop or reduce hours sooner.

Before you make any filing decision based on specific dollar amounts, verify current-year figures at SSA.gov. Bend points, COLA percentages, and maximum taxable earnings change each year.

Key reminders: Your benefit is based on 35 years of earnings. If you have fewer than 35 years, zeros are included. Your PIA is calculated with a progressive formula that uses bend points, and those bend points change each year. Your Social Security statement is the fastest way to spot missing or underreported earnings. Corrections are usually simpler to handle before you file.

Most common mistakes: Assuming your Social Security statement is automatically correct. Skipping a check for missing or underreported years. Filing for benefits without reviewing your earnings history. Waiting until after claiming to discover and fix errors.

Next steps: Log in to SSA.gov and pull your full earnings history. Compare it to your own records. If you find a mismatch, start gathering documentation and contact the SSA while the paper trail is still available.

2

BEFORE YOU CLAIM: CHOOSING THE RIGHT FILING AGE FOR YOUR SITUATION

The decision about when to start collecting Social Security shapes your monthly income for the rest of your life. Once you file, your benefit is mostly locked in. You cannot come back years later and say, "I wish I had waited," and expect the system to rewind. That is why this choice deserves more than a gut feeling or a quick chat with a coworker who retired last spring. It deserves a clear look at your finances, your health, your family situation, and what you want your later years to look like.

You now know how your benefit is built from your highest 35 years of earnings, your Average Indexed Monthly Earnings (AIME), and the progressive formula that produces your Primary Insurance Amount (PIA). The next question is simpler to ask than it is to answer: at what age should you actually start taking the benefit?

It depends, and the details matter. This chapter walks through the three main claiming windows, shows how each one changes your monthly check, introduces break-even analysis so you can see the tradeoffs in plain numbers, and then follows a real-life scenario to show how the decision plays out over time.

Early Retirement at 62: Pros and Cons

The earliest age you can claim Social Security retirement benefits is 62. A lot of people file then because they can, because they have stopped working, or because they need the income right away. Claiming early puts cash in your account sooner. The tradeoff is built into the rules, and it is permanent.

How the reduction works. When you claim before your Full Retirement Age (FRA), the Social Security Administration (SSA) reduces your monthly benefit for each month you file early. The size of the cut depends on the number of months between your filing date and your FRA.

For the first 36 months before your FRA, benefits are reduced by 5/9 of one % per month. For any additional months beyond 36, which applies if your FRA is 67 and you claim at 62, the reduction is 5/12 of one % per month.

In plain English, if your FRA is 67, claiming at 62 means filing 60 months early. The total reduction is about 30%. If your full benefit at 67 would have been $2,000 per month, claiming at 62 drops it to roughly $1,400 per month. That lower number stays with you for life. Future Cost-of-Living Adjustments (COLAs) are applied to the reduced benefit amount. So you do not "catch up" to the full benefit later.

Claiming at 62 vs FRA vs 70

This example shows how the age you claim Social Security can permanently change your monthly benefit. The amounts below are based on a Primary Insurance Amount (PIA) of $2,000 at Full Retirement Age (FRA).

Claiming Age	Monthly Benefit	Change from FRA	What It Means
62	**$1,400/month**	**30% lower**	You receive smaller checks for life, but start collecting earlier.
67 (FRA)	**$2,000/month**	**Baseline**	You receive 100% of your Primary Insurance Amount.
70	**$2,480/month**	**24% higher**	You receive the largest monthly benefit, but must wait longer to start.

What This Comparison Shows

- Claiming at 62 reduces the monthly benefit permanently.
- Waiting until FRA gives the full unreduced benefit.
- Delaying until 70 increases the benefit through delayed retirement credits.

Quick Reminder

- FRA stands for Full Retirement Age.
- This is a simplified example for illustration only.

Actual benefit amounts vary based on your earnings history, claiming age, and Social Security rules.

When early claiming may make sense. Filing at 62 can be a reasonable choice in some situations. If you lost your job and do not have enough savings to bridge the gap, if your health points to a shorter life expectancy, or if you have other income and want the flexibility of smaller checks sooner, early claiming can do its job. Some people also claim early while a spouse keeps working, so they can pull less from retirement accounts.

The long-term income impact. The tradeoff is straightforward: start early, and you get more checks, but every check is smaller. Over a long retirement, especially one that runs into your 80s or 90s, the cumulative gap can get big. A $600 monthly difference over 20 years is $144,000 less in benefits. Live longer than that, and the gap keeps widening.

Here is the part people miss: early claiming is a permanent reduction with no reset button. If you claim at 62, you do not later "switch" to your full benefit at 67. The reduced amount is your benefit for life, adjusted only by annual COLAs.

Full Retirement Age and Its Importance

Your Full Retirement Age (FRA) is the age when you receive 100% of your PIA. Think of your PIA as the baseline. Everything else, whether claiming early or delaying, is measured against it.

FRA by birth year. Your FRA depends on the year you were born. For people born between 1943 and 1954, the Full Retirement Age is 66. For those born in 1955 through 1959, the FRA increases by two months per year. For those born in 1960 or later, the FRA is 67. Most readers of this guide will have an FRA of either 66 and some months, or 67.

Full Retirement Age by Birth Year

Your Full Retirement Age (FRA) is the age when you are eligible to receive 100% of your Primary Insurance Amount (PIA).

Year You Were Born	Your Full Retirement Age (FRA)
1943 - 1954	66
1955	66 and 2 months
1956	66 and 4 months
1957	66 and 6 months
1958	66 and 8 months
1959	66 and 10 months
1960 and later	67

Important: If you were born on January 1, use the earlier birth year. If you were born on the 1st of the month, your FRA is the same as those born in the previous month.

Why FRA matters so much, FRA is the anchor point for every benefit calculation. Claim before the FRA, and your benefit is permanently reduced from that baseline. Claim after the FRA, and your benefit is permanently increased above it. Knowing your FRA is step one for any claiming strategy.

The earnings test disappears at FRA. If you plan to keep working while collecting Social Security, FRA is a line that matters. Before FRA, the SSA applies an earnings test that can temporarily withhold benefits if your wages exceed certain limits. The earnings test for Social Security benefits disappears at the Full Retirement Age. At that point, you can earn any amount from work without reducing your Social Security payment. (The next chapter covers the earnings test in detail.)

So if you are still working full-time and earning above the annual limit, claiming before the FRA can mean some benefits are withheld. For many people in that situation, waiting until at least the FRA is the cleaner move, unless there is a specific need or a strategy that makes early claiming worth it.

One hundred % of your PIA. Claiming at the FRA means you get what the formula says you earned. No penalty. No bonus. Just the full amount based on your 35 best years of indexed earnings, run through the bend-point formula described in the previous chapter. For plenty of retirees, the FRA is the natural claiming point because it is the moment the system pays their baseline benefit with no timing adjustment.

Delayed Retirement Credits: The 8% Bonus

Wait past your FRA to claim, and the SSA adds delayed retirement credits. Each month you postpone increases your benefit. The annual rate is 8% per year, calculated monthly, which is about two-thirds of one % per month.

How the credits accumulate. If your FRA is 67 and you wait until 68, your monthly benefit is 8% higher than your PIA. Wait until 69, and it is 16 % higher. Hold off until 70, and it is 24% higher. Using the earlier $2,000 PIA example, delaying to 70 raises the benefit to $2,480 per month. Compare that to about $1,400 per month at 62, and you are looking at a $1,080 monthly difference, every month, for as long as you receive benefits.

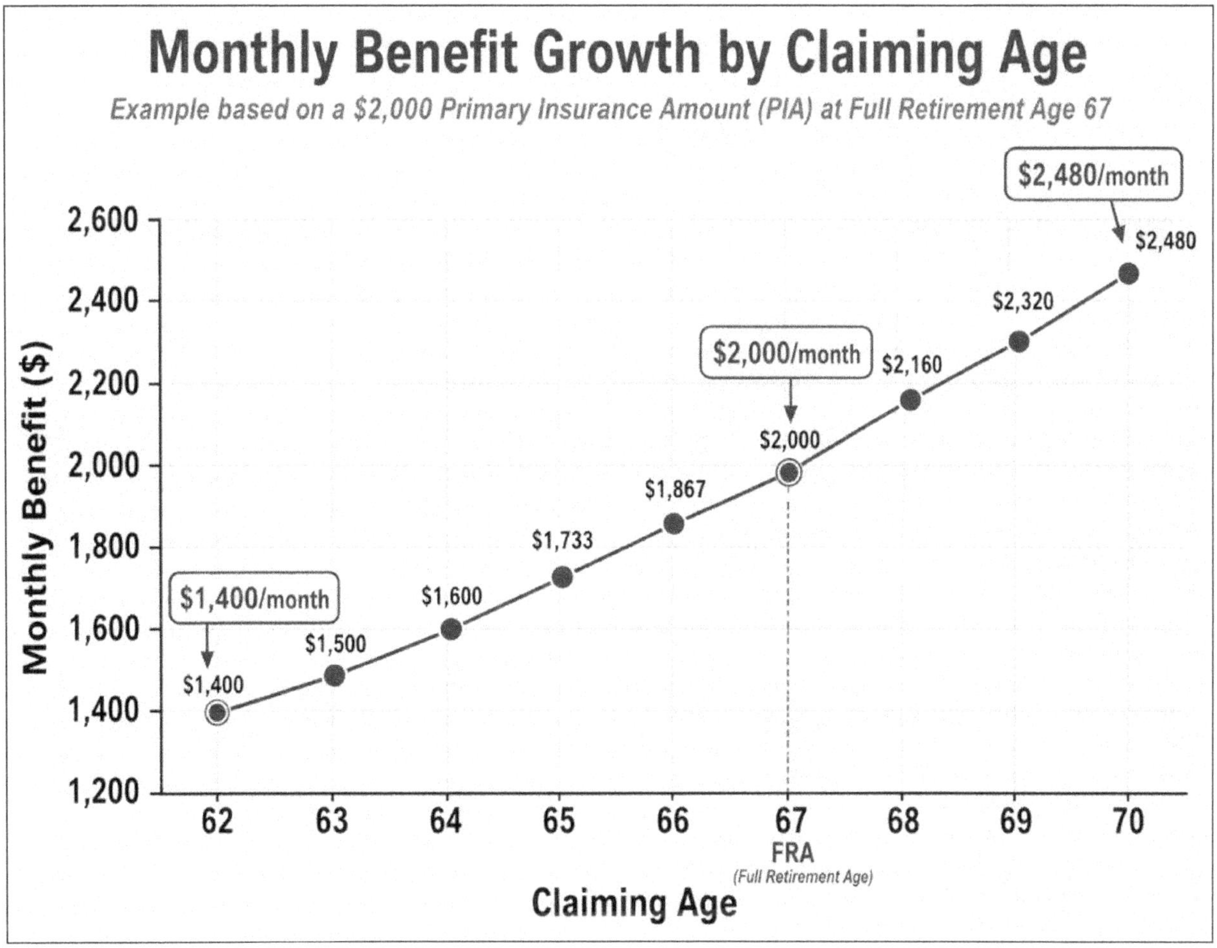

The compound effect over time. Delayed retirement credits also change what happens with COLAs. Once benefits start, everyone gets the same percentage COLA. But starting from a higher base means each COLA is worth more in dollars. Over 20 or 25 years, that gap can become hard to ignore.

Take two people with identical work histories. One claims at 62 and receives $1,400 per month. The other waits until 70 and receives $2,480 per month. After 10 years of 2.5% average annual COLAs, the early claimer receives about $1,792 per month, while the delayed claimer receives about $3,175 per month. The monthly difference has grown from $1,080 to roughly $1,383, and it keeps widening each year.

When delay stops paying. Delayed retirement credits stop at age 70. There is no benefit to waiting past your 70th birthday to claim. If you hit 70 and have not filed, apply. Waiting longer will not raise your benefit.

One more point that often gets overlooked: this 8% annual increase is written into the program rules. You do not have to take on market risk to get it.

When delaying may not be the right choice. Delaying tends to work best if you are in good health, expect to live past your late 70s or early 80s, and can cover expenses from other sources, such as savings, a pension, a spouse's income, or part-time work, while you wait. If a serious condition shortens your expected lifespan, or if you cannot cover basic bills without Social Security, waiting until 70 can mean fewer total dollars over your lifetime.

Break-Even Analysis for Different Ages

Break-even analysis answers a practical question: at what age does delaying start to pay off? Put another way, how long do you need to live before the larger monthly check from waiting overtakes the total dollars you would have collected by claiming earlier?

How break-even works. The idea is simple. Claim early, and you get smaller checks for more months. Delay and you get larger checks, but you start later. At some point, the delayed strategy catches up to the early strategy and then moves ahead. That crossover point is the break-even age.

Let's use a specific example. Assume your PIA is $2,000 at an FRA of 67.

If you claim at 62, you receive about $1,400 per month. By the time you reach 67, you have collected around $84,000 (60 months multiplied by $1,400).

If you wait until 67, you start at $2,000 per month, with nothing collected up to that point. At age 67, you are behind by $84,000. After that, though, you are receiving $600 more per month than the early claimer. It takes roughly 140 months, about 11.7 years, to close that gap. That puts the break-even point around age 78 to 79.

Now compare claiming at 67 versus 70. Delay to 70 and you receive $2,480 per month. From 67 to 70, you forgo $72,000 in benefits (36 months multiplied by $2,000). After 70, you collect $480 more per month than you would have at 67. It takes about 150 months (12.5 years) to make up the difference, placing the break-even point around age 82 to 83.

These are simplified calculations. They do not include COLAs, taxes, or what you might do with money received earlier, like investing it or using it to avoid withdrawals from a portfolio. Still, the basic math gives you a solid starting point.

YOUR SOCIAL SECURITY NUMBERS

Use this worksheet to record your key Social Security benefit numbers so you can compare claiming age options and plan with confidence.

How to Use This Worksheet

Find these numbers on your Social Security Statement (ssa.gov/myaccount) or benefit estimate (ssa.gov/benefits/retirement/estimator). Enter the amounts below for easy reference and comparison.

1. YOUR BASIC INFORMATION

Your Name:	
Date of Birth:	
Full Retirement Age (FRA):	
Today's Date:	

2. YOUR SOCIAL SECURITY BENEFIT AMOUNTS

(Monthly amounts before any deductions)

Claiming Age	Description	Your Monthly Benefit Amount
62 **Age 62**	Early Retirement Benefit (typically reduced)	$__________
67 **Age 67 (FRA)**	Full Retirement Age Benefit (100% of your Primary Insurance Amount)	$__________
70 **Age 70**	Delayed Retirement Benefit (maximum – includes delayed retirement credits)	$__________

3. YOUR NOTES

Use this space to note questions, reminders, or anything you want to consider.

TIP: Your benefit may change over time due to earnings, cost-of-living adjustments (COLAs), or changes in the law. Check your numbers at least once a year.

Life expectancy considerations. According to SSA actuarial tables, a 65-year-old today can expect to live to roughly age 82 (men) or about 85 (women), with wide variation based on individual factors. Women tend to live longer than men on average. If you are healthy at 62, the odds of living past the typical break-even range, around 78 to 83, depending on which ages you compare, are often better than people assume.

SSA actuarial tables also show that roughly one in four 65-year-old men and about one in three 65-year-old women will live past age 90, around 30 % combined. If you are in that group, the income advantage of delaying can become substantial. The farther you live past the break-even point, the more the delayed strategy pulls ahead.

Health status factors. Break-even analysis assumes you have no personal information about your health. In real life, you usually do. A family history of longevity, strong current health, and no major chronic conditions tend to support delaying. A life-shortening diagnosis, or a pattern of close relatives dying in their late 60s or early 70s, pushes the math toward claiming earlier.

You cannot forecast the future perfectly. But you can stop guessing and use break-even analysis to frame the decision.

What break-even analysis doesn't capture. Break-even analysis focuses on lifetime dollars collected. It does not fully capture the value of a higher monthly income later, when you might have fewer resources, higher medical costs, or less ability to earn money. For many retirees, the monthly amount matters more than the grand total. A larger check can reduce the risk of running short late in life, especially after age 80, when other income sources may be smaller than expected.

Mistake Alert and Real-Life Scenario

Mistake Alert: Filing for Social Security at 62 without running the numbers for your situation is one of the most common and expensive retirement planning errors. People file because they can, because a friend did, or because they assume the benefit will increase later. It will not. The reduction is permanent. Before you file at any age, calculate your break-even point, think about your health and family history, and decide whether you can cover expenses through other sources while you wait.

Real-Life Scenario: Robert's Claiming Decision

Robert is 62. He recently left a manufacturing job and is considering filing for Social Security right away. His PIA at his Full Retirement Age (67) would be $2,200 per month. He is healthy, takes no medications, and both of his parents lived into their late 80s.

If Robert claims at 62, his benefit drops by 30% to about $1,540 per month. He likes the idea of income right now and figures, "I've been paying in for 40 years. I want my money."

Here is how it looks over time.

By age 70, Robert has collected about $148,000 in benefits (96 months multiplied by $1,540). If he had waited until 67, he would have collected $79,200 by age 70 (36 months multiplied by $2,200). At that point, early claiming is still ahead by about $69,000.

Around age 79, the person who waited until 67 catches up. From then on, the full-benefit claimer receives $660 more each month than Robert does. By age 85, the cumulative advantage of waiting has grown to about $50,000. By 90, it approaches $90,000.

If Robert had waited until 70, his benefit would have been $2,728 per month, a 24% increase over his PIA. The break-even point compared to claiming at 62 lands around age 80 to 81. Given Robert's health and family history, living past 80 is not a stretch.

What Robert didn't consider. Robert also has a spouse, Lorraine, who earned less over her career. If Robert dies first, survivor benefits are based on the deceased spouse's benefit amount, which reflects their Primary Insurance Amount and the age at which they claimed (the monthly amount they were receiving, or were entitled to receive, at the time of death). By claiming early, Robert locked in a lower benefit, which means Lorraine's potential survivor benefit is also lower. If Robert had delayed, Lorraine could receive a larger monthly survivor check for the rest of her life. (Survivor benefits are covered in detail in a later chapter.)

What Robert's story shows. Claiming early felt right in the moment. But without doing a break-even check, weighing his health outlook, or thinking through the survivor-benefit angle, Robert likely gave up meaningful long-term income. Early claiming can be the right call. It just should not be an automatic one.

Chapter Checklist and Verification Tips

Use this checklist to evaluate your own claiming-age decision before you file. There is no single "right" age for everyone, but there is a right way to think it through.

Log in to your my Social Security account at SSA.gov and review your benefit estimates at 62, FRA, and 70

1. Identify your exact Full Retirement Age based on your birth year
2. Calculate the dollar difference between your benefit at 62, FRA, and 70
3. Estimate your break-even age for each comparison (62 vs. FRA, 62 vs. 70, FRA vs. 70)
4. Assess your current health honestly: do you have chronic conditions or a family history that affects longevity?
5. Consider whether you plan to keep working past 62 (if so, the earnings test may withhold early benefits)
6. If married, evaluate how your claiming decision affects your spouse's potential survivor benefit
7. Review other income sources: can you cover living expenses without Social Security if you delay?

8. If you have a pension, 401(k), IRA, or other savings, consider whether drawing from those first while delaying Social Security produces a higher total lifetime income

Use the SSA Retirement Estimator at SSA.gov to run scenarios based on different claiming ages and stop-work dates

Consider consulting a fee-only financial planner if your situation involves spousal coordination, survivor planning, or complex tax considerations.

Verification tips:

Benefit estimates on your Social Security statement assume you keep working at your current income until the age shown. If you plan to retire earlier or cut your hours, your actual benefit may be lower than the estimate. For better numbers, run projections using the SSA's Detailed Calculator or Retirement Estimator.

All dollar amounts, reduction percentages, and delayed retirement credit rates in this chapter should be checked against current SSA.gov figures. The basic structure has been stable for years (about a 30% reduction at 62 for someone with an FRA of 67, 8% per year in delayed credits, and credits stopping at 70), but confirm the details before you file.

If you are on the fence about delaying, write out your monthly expenses, compare them to your non-Social Security income, and answer one question: Can you cover the gap for three to eight years while your benefit grows?

Key reminders: Claiming at 62 means a permanent reduction of up to 30% (for those with an FRA of 67). Claiming at the FRA gives you 100% of your PIA. Delaying past the FRA adds 8% per year in credits, up to age 70. Break-even math often shows delaying pays off if you live past your late 70s to early 80s.

Most common mistakes: Filing at 62 without understanding the permanent reduction. Ignoring how your claiming age affects a spouse's survivor benefit. Assuming the SSA will increase your benefit later if you claimed early. Waiting past 70, when no additional credits build.

Next steps: Pull your benefit estimates at 62, FRA, and 70 from your Social Security statement. Calculate your break-even ages. Take a hard look at your health and your budget. If you are married, run the survivor-benefit implications before you decide. Then pick an age and file accordingly.

3

WORKING WHILE CLAIMING: HOW EARNINGS CAN AFFECT YOUR CHECKS

A lot of people assume that once they file for Social Security, the monthly deposit shows up like clockwork, no matter what else is happening in their financial life. For retirees who have fully stopped working, that is basically true. But if you are still earning income from a job or self-employment while collecting benefits before your Full Retirement Age (FRA), the Social Security Administration (SSA) applies rules that can temporarily reduce, or even stop, your monthly payments. These rules catch people off guard every year. The surprise usually arrives as a letter saying benefits were withheld, or an unexpected overpayment notice that asks for money back.

What's easy to miss is that the earnings test has more moving parts than the headline makes it sound. Benefits withheld now are not automatically gone. They can feed back into your payment later. If you understand the mechanics, you can time work changes, estimate cash flow more realistically, and avoid the kind of "wait, what?" moment that can throw off an otherwise solid retirement plan.

How the Earnings Test Works

The earnings test applies only if you are collecting Social Security retirement benefits and you have not yet reached your Full Retirement Age. Once you hit the FRA, the test disappears. You can earn any amount from work without reducing your Social Security payment. The previous chapter touched on this. Here is what it looks like in real life.

Before FRA: the income limit. Each year, the SSA sets an annual earnings limit for people who are under the FRA for the entire year. If your earnings from work exceed that limit, the SSA withholds $1 in benefits for every $2 you earn above the threshold. For example, if the annual limit is $24,480 and you earn $34,480, you are $10,000 over the limit. The SSA withholds $5,000 from your benefits that year. (Verify the current-year earnings limit at SSA.gov; it adjusts annually with inflation.)

The year you reach the FRA: a higher limit. In the calendar year you turn your FRA, a more generous limit applies for the months before your birthday month. The withholding rate also drops. Instead of $1 for every $2 over the limit, the SSA withholds $1 for every $3 you earn above the higher threshold.

Monthly versus annual application. This is especially helpful if you retire mid-year after earning a large salary in the first few months. Under the monthly test, you can receive benefits for any month you are "retired" under SSA rules, even if your total annual earnings are high. That prevents someone who earned $90,000 between January and June from losing benefits for the rest of the year after they have fully stopped working. After the first year, the SSA typically switches to the annual test.

What this means for your check. If you claim Social Security at 62 or 63 while still working full-time at a salary well above the earnings limit, a significant portion of your benefit, possibly all of it, can be withheld. Many people in this situation effectively receive no monthly payment despite having filed. That does not mean the money is gone forever, as explained in the Give-back Provision section below. It does mean your cash flow during those years may look very different from what you expected.

What Counts as Earnings

The earnings test does not apply to all income. It looks specifically at earned income from work. Knowing what counts and what doesn't can save you a lot of unnecessary stress and help you plan with cleaner numbers.

W-2 wages. If you work for an employer, your gross wages count toward the earnings test. The SSA uses what you earn in the year, regardless of when you receive the paycheck.

Self-employment net profits. This is your gross revenue minus allowable business expenses. For the monthly test in the first year, the SSA also looks at whether you performed "substantial services" in your business during a given month, which generally means more than 45 hours of work, or 15 to 45 hours in a highly skilled occupation.

What does not count. Several common income sources are excluded from the earnings test entirely:

- Pension payments
- 401(k), IRA, or other retirement account withdrawals
- Investment income (dividends, interest, capital gains)
- Annuity payments
- Social Security benefits themselves

- Government benefits, such as veterans' payments

This distinction matters. If you have $50,000 in investment income and $15,000 in part-time wages, only the $15,000 counts toward the earnings test. The investments do not trigger withholding. Similarly, if you withdraw $30,000 from your IRA to cover living expenses, that withdrawal has no effect on the earnings test. (It may affect taxes on your Social Security benefits, which is covered in a later chapter, but it does not trigger the earnings test.)

WHAT COUNTS AS EARNINGS vs WHAT DOES NOT

Social Security uses your taxable earnings to calculate your benefit.
Here's what does and does not count toward your earnings record.

WHAT COUNTS AS EARNINGS		WHAT DOES NOT COUNT AS EARNINGS	
Item	**Examples**	**Item**	**Examples**
Wages from Employment	Salary, hourly wages, bonuses, commissions, tips (that are subject to Social Security tax)	**Gifts and Inheritance**	Money you receive as a gift or inheritance
Self-Employment Income	Net earnings from self-employment (sole proprietorships, partnerships, independent contractors)	**Investment Income**	Interest, dividends, capital gains, rents, royalties, and annuities
Certain Government Employment	Wages from most federal, state, and local government jobs covered by Social Security	**Government Benefits**	Social Security benefits, unemployment benefits, workers' compensation, public assistance
Work Outside the U.S.	Wages from work performed outside the U.S. for an American employer or certain foreign employers	**Alimony and Child Support**	Alimony payments and child support payments
Some Types of Seafaring Work	Certain seafaring earnings that are subject to Social Security tax	**Employer-Paid Fringe Benefits**	Health insurance, group-term life insurance, pension contributions, and other fringe benefits

IMPORTANT NOTES:

- Only earnings that are subject to Social Security tax are included in your earnings record.
- Your earnings record is based on W-2s and self-employment tax returns reported to Social Security.

Review your official earnings record at SSA.gov/myaccount to verify your reported earnings.

The Giveback Provision

This is the piece most people don't hear when the earnings test comes up: benefits withheld before FRA are not necessarily gone for good. The SSA recalculates your benefit once you reach Full Retirement Age, and months that were fully withheld can be credited back through a higher monthly payment going forward.

How the recalculation works. When you claimed before the FRA, your benefit was reduced for early filing. Each month you actually received that reduced benefit counts as a month of early claiming. Months in which your entire benefit was withheld due to the earnings test are handled differently. At the FRA, the SSA reviews how many months were withheld and adjusts your ongoing benefit upward to reflect them.

In plain English: if you claimed at 62 but the earnings test withheld 24 months of benefits over the next five years, the SSA recalculates your benefit at FRA as if you had claimed two years later than you actually did. Your monthly payment going forward increases to reflect those 24 months of non-payment.

What this means for your long-term income. The giveback provision does not cut you a lump-sum check at FRA. Instead, it raises your monthly benefit for the rest of your life. Over a long retirement, that higher monthly amount can recover most, and sometimes all, of what was withheld. If you live well past the FRA, the difference adds up.

Credit for additional earnings. There is a second upside to working while collecting. If your current earnings are higher than one of the 35 years used in your original benefit calculation, the SSA can swap in the new, higher year. That raises your Average Indexed Monthly Earnings (AIME) and can increase your Primary Insurance Amount (PIA). The SSA reviews this annually. So working in your early 60s, even if some benefits are temporarily withheld, can boost your future benefit in two ways: via the giveback provision and via stronger lifetime earnings.

A practical way to think about it. The earnings test is a deferral, not a forfeiture. You are, in effect, postponing some early-claiming payments so you can receive a higher monthly amount later. If you plan to keep working past 62 with strong earnings, that means the "penalty" for claiming early is partly offset over time. It does not wipe out the early-claiming reduction, but it can make the outcome less lopsided than people assume.

Strategies for Managing Work and Benefits

Knowing the rules is one thing. Making them work with your paycheck, your plans, and your tolerance for paperwork is another. Here are several strategies that can help you manage the interaction between work income and Social Security benefits.

Timing your work reduction. If you plan to scale back from full-time work, look at how the timing lines up with the earnings-test limits. Dropping below the annual limit in a given year means no benefits are withheld that year. If you are 64 and plan to cut to part-time at 65, mapping out projected earnings year by year lets you estimate whether, and how much, would be withheld. Some people reduce hours a year earlier than planned, specifically to stay under the limit and keep their full monthly check.

Consulting and contract income considerations. If you are moving from a salaried role into consulting or freelance work, the timing of when you invoice and when you receive payment can affect which calendar year income falls into. You cannot fabricate timing just to dodge the rules, but legitimate business decisions, like when to take on projects or when to bill, can change your annual total. Self-employed individuals also have the monthly services test available during their first year of benefits, which can help if consulting work is clustered in certain months.

Part-time versus full-time. A common approach is to claim Social Security at 62 or 63 while working part-time, intentionally keeping earnings near or below the annual limit. That can provide both a paycheck and a Social Security payment without triggering withholding. The trade-off is straightforward: part-time income is usually lower than your old full-time salary, and your benefit is still reduced for early claiming. Still, for people who want to step down gradually rather than stop working overnight, the combined income can be steadier.

Deferring the claim entirely. If you are earning well above the limit and expect to keep working for several more years, claiming before the FRA may not help much. If most or all of your monthly check will be withheld, you may prefer to wait. Delaying the claim means your benefit grows through delayed retirement credits (8% per year past the FRA, as covered in the previous chapter), and it avoids the back-and-forth of withholding and recalculation later.

Coordinating with a spouse. If one spouse plans to keep working and the other does not, the non-working spouse can claim without earnings-test concerns while the working spouse delays. That gives the household some Social Security income while allowing the higher earner's benefit to grow. Spousal strategies are covered in depth in the next chapter, but the earnings test is another reason to think carefully about who claims when.

Mistake Alert and Real-Life Scenario

Mistake Alert: Claiming Social Security while working full-time at a salary well above the earnings limit is one of the most common sources of confusion and frustration. People file expecting a monthly check, then receive a letter from the SSA saying benefits were withheld. Some end up owing money back because they underestimated their annual earnings. Before you claim while still working, estimate your expected earnings for the year and compare them to the current earnings limit. If you are significantly over the limit, run the math on how much would be withheld and ask yourself whether claiming now actually helps your cash flow.

Real-Life Scenario: Karen's Consulting Income Surprise

Karen is 63. She left her corporate marketing job at the end of last year and filed for Social Security in January, expecting her monthly benefit of $1,680 to supplement her savings. She planned to take on some freelance consulting to stay active and earn extra income, "maybe $30,000 or so."

By October, Karen's consulting contracts had brought in $48,000 for the year, and she expected another $10,000 or so before year-end. The annual earnings limit was $24,480 (verify the current-year amount at SSA.gov as it adjusts annually). Karen was already $23,520 over the limit, and on pace to be roughly $35,000 over by December. The SSA withholds $1 for every $2 you earn above the limit, which would mean about $16,750 in benefits withheld for the year. That would effectively wipe out more than ten months of her $1,680 monthly payments. When the SSA learned about her consulting income, they suspended her benefit payments for the rest of the year and notified her that the months she had already been paid would create an overpayment she would need to repay.

Karen was surprised and frustrated. She felt she had lost money. What actually happened is less dramatic: those withheld months will be credited back at FRA through the giveback provision. Her monthly benefit from the FRA onward will be higher than it would have been if she had collected every month at the reduced early-claiming rate.

What Karen could have done differently. Karen had several options. She could have delayed her Social Security claim until her consulting income settled at a lower level. She could have tracked her earnings month by month and slowed her consulting in the second half of the year to stay closer to the limit. Or she could have treated the withholding as a planned trade-off, knowing the giveback provision would raise her benefit later.

Income management strategies. Karen's situation is a good example of why tracking earnings throughout the year matters. If you are self-employed or doing contract work, set up a simple spreadsheet to monitor cumulative earnings against the annual limit. As you approach the threshold, you can decide whether to take on additional work or push a new project into the next calendar year through legitimate contract and billing timing.

Chapter Checklist and Verification Tips

Use this checklist to manage the interaction between your work income and Social Security benefits.

- Verify the current-year earnings limit at SSA.gov (the amount changes annually)
- Estimate your projected earnings for each year you plan to work while collecting benefits before the FRA
- Determine whether the monthly test applies during your first year of benefits
- Identify which of your income sources count toward the earnings test and which are excluded
- Track cumulative earned income monthly so you know when you are approaching the limit
- Understand that withheld benefits are recalculated at FRA, increasing your monthly payment going forward
- If self-employed, monitor both net profits and hours of substantial services
- If you are in the year you reach the FRA, check whether the higher limit and lower withholding rate apply
- Consider whether delaying your claim makes more sense than filing and having most benefits withheld

- Report changes in your work status or expected earnings to the SSA promptly to avoid overpayments

Verification tips:

The annual earnings limit, the higher limit for the year you reach FRA, and the monthly threshold all change each year. Check SSA.gov for current figures before making decisions based on specific dollar amounts mentioned anywhere, including in this guide.

If you receive an overpayment notice from the SSA because your earnings exceeded what you reported, respond quickly. You can request a repayment plan or, in some cases, request a waiver if repayment would cause financial hardship.

Key reminders: The earnings test only applies before the FRA. Only earned income from work counts. Benefits withheld are not permanently lost; they can increase your monthly payment at the FRA through the giveback provision. Once you reach the FRA, you can earn any amount without reducing your Social Security.

Most common mistakes: Claiming early while working full-time and being surprised by withholding. Failing to track income throughout the year. Confusing investment income or retirement withdrawals with earned income. Assuming withheld benefits are gone forever.

Next steps: Pull the current-year earnings limit from SSA.gov. Estimate your earned income for the next one to three years. If you plan to work while collecting, compare what happens if you claim now versus waiting. If you are already collecting and still working, start tracking monthly earnings against the annual limit so you see problems before the SSA does.

4

SPOUSAL BENEFITS: HOW COUPLES CAN COORDINATE FOR MORE LIFETIME SECURITY

A married couple has two Social Security records, two claiming decisions, and two timelines to juggle. When those decisions are made in isolation, each spouse files when it feels right for them personally. Coordinate the timing, and the household can often collect more total income over a full retirement. The difference can easily reach tens of thousands of dollars over a couple's lifetime.

This chapter explains how spousal benefits work, how the math determines what you receive, and how couples can time their claims to support both spouses through retirement and widowhood. Whether you earned similar incomes, had a wide earnings gap, or have an age difference that complicates timing, the rules that follow will help you work through the decision as a team.

How Spousal Benefits Are Calculated

Social Security allows one spouse to receive a benefit based on the other spouse's earnings record. That is the spousal benefit. It exists so that a lower-earning (or non-working) spouse can still receive retirement income tied to the household's work history.

The 50% rule. The maximum spousal benefit is 50% of the higher-earning spouse's Primary Insurance Amount (PIA). Your PIA is the monthly benefit you would receive at your Full Retirement Age (FRA). If your spouse's PIA is $2,400 per month, the maximum spousal benefit available to you is $1,200 per month, assuming you claim at your own FRA.

That 50% is based on the worker's PIA, regardless of when the worker actually files. If your spouse delays past the FRA and earns delayed retirement credits, those credits increase the worker's check but do not raise the spousal benefit above 50% of the original PIA.

Reduction for early claiming. If you claim a spousal benefit before your own FRA, the benefit is permanently reduced. The reduction works much like the one described in the earlier chapter on claiming ages. For each month you start before your FRA, the amount is reduced. File at 62 with a FRA of 67, and the spousal benefit drops from 50% of your spouse's PIA to roughly 32.5 %. That reduction stays in place for life.

Put simply, waiting longer (up to your FRA) gets you closer to the full 50%. But spousal benefits have one important limitation. They do not grow after the FRA. Delayed retirement credits do not apply to spousal benefits, so waiting past your FRA does not increase the spousal amount above 50%.

Own benefit versus spousal benefit. The Social Security Administration (SSA) does not let you choose whichever benefit you prefer. When you file, the SSA looks at both your own retirement benefit (based on your work record) and the spousal benefit available from your spouse's record, then pays the higher amount using its rules. If your own PIA is $900 and your spousal benefit would be $1,200, you end up with $1,200. If your own PIA is $1,400 and the spousal benefit is $1,200, you receive $1,400 based on your own record.

OWN BENEFIT vs SPOUSAL BENEFIT

You may be eligible for retirement benefits based on your own work record and/or your spouse's work record. Here's how they compare.

FEATURE	OWN BENEFIT (Based on Your Work Record)	SPOUSAL BENEFIT (Based on Your Spouse's Work Record)
What It Is	The benefit amount you earn based on your own lifetime of Social Security–covered earnings.	A benefit you may receive based on your spouse's work record.
How It's Calculated	Based on your average indexed monthly earnings and the 90% / 32% / 15% formula.	Up to 50% of your spouse's Primary Insurance Amount (PIA) at their Full Retirement Age (FRA). (Reduced if claimed early.)
Who Can Receive It	You, based on your own earnings record.	You, if you are: • Married for at least 1 year (some exceptions apply) • Age 62 or older • Not entitled to a higher benefit on your own record
When You Can Claim	As early as age 62. Full amount at your Full Retirement Age (FRA). Increased if you delay to age 70.	As early as age 62. Full 50% amount at your spouse's FRA. Reduced if claimed before your spouse's FRA.
Amount You Receive	Could be more, less, or the same as a spousal benefit—depending on your earnings history.	Up to 50% of your spouse's PIA at their FRA. If you also qualify on your own record, Social Security pays the higher total benefit.
Special Notes	If you qualify for both, you will receive the higher of the two amounts.	Does not reduce the benefit your spouse receives. You do not need your spouse's permission to claim.

KEY TAKEAWAY:
Always compare your own benefit and potential spousal benefit before claiming. You will receive whichever amount is higher.

Divorced? You may be eligible for a divorced-spouse benefit under certain rules. See Chapter 6.

One requirement matters for planning: in most cases, you cannot receive a spousal benefit until the higher-earning spouse has filed for their own retirement benefit. That timing rule is a big part of the coordination strategy, which we cover next.

Claiming Strategies for Married Couples

Once both spouses understand the spousal benefit rules, it becomes easier to coordinate filing dates and raise the household's total retirement income. The goal is to treat Social Security as one combined income stream and look at what both spouses will receive over the full length of both retirements.

Sequential claiming approaches. A common strategy is to have the lower-earning spouse file first while the higher-earning spouse delays. The appeal is straightforward. When the lower earner files at 62 or at FRA, the household starts receiving some Social Security income right away. At the same time, the higher earner waits and earns delayed retirement credits, increasing their benefit by 8% per year between FRA and 70 (as described in the earlier chapter on claiming ages). When the higher earner files at 70, the household payment usually jumps.

This approach does two things. It creates cash flow earlier without giving up the largest possible check on the higher earner's record. It also helps build the biggest possible survivor benefit later, since survivor benefits are based on what the deceased spouse was receiving (or was entitled to receive).

Income gap considerations. The wider the gap between the two spouses' PIAs, the more there is to gain from coordinating. If one spouse has a PIA of $2,600 and the other has a PIA of $800, the spousal benefit for the lower earner (up to $1,300 at FRA) can be far more than their own record provides. In a gap like that, having the higher earner delay to 70 can raise the household's monthly income and increase the eventual survivor benefit for the remaining spouse.

When both spouses earned similar amounts, spousal benefits often matter less because each spouse's own benefit is higher than 50 % of the other's PIA. In those households, coordination tends to be more about timing and survivor protection than about unlocking a larger spousal amount.

Timing coordination benefits. The most powerful result of coordination is in the planning. A few principles tend to hold:

- The higher earner's delay can increase both the monthly benefit and the survivor benefit that the remaining spouse may rely on later.
- The lower earner's earlier filing can provide income during the waiting period and may not reduce total lifetime dollars by much if their own benefit is modest.
- Having both spouses file on the same day at 62 often leaves the most money on the table, especially when one spouse could have delayed.

Spousal Benefit Planning Worksheet

Use this worksheet to compare each spouse's own benefit, possible spousal benefits, and different claiming combinations.

1. Record Each Spouse's Key Numbers

	Spouse A	Spouse B
Name		
Birth Year		
Full Retirement Age (FRA)		
Primary Insurance Amount (PIA)		
Estimated Benefit at 62		
Estimated Benefit at FRA		
Estimated Benefit at 70		

2. Compare Own Benefit vs Spousal Benefit

Higher earner: ______________________

Higher earner's PIA: ______________________

50% of higher earner's PIA: ______________________

Spouse A own PIA: ______________________

Spouse A possible spousal amount: ______________________

Spouse B own PIA: ______________________

Spouse B possible spousal amount: ______________________

Which benefit appears higher for each spouse? ______________________

3. Test Different Claiming Scenarios

Scenario	Spouse A Claiming Age	Spouse B Claiming Age	Estimated Monthly Household Income	Notes
Both claim at 62				
Both claim at FRA				
Lower earner claims first, higher earner delays				
Higher earner delays to 70				
Custom strategy				

4. Survivor Planning Check

If Spouse A dies first, surviving spouse may receive: ______________________

If Spouse B dies first, surviving spouse may receive: ______________________

Which claiming strategy best protects the surviving spouse? ______________________

Does delaying the higher earner's benefit improve survivor protection? ______________________

5. Action Checklist

- ☐ Pull both Social Security statements from SSA.gov
- ☐ Confirm each spouse's PIA
- ☐ Identify the higher earner
- ☐ Compare own benefit vs spousal benefit
- ☐ Review estimated benefits at 62, FRA, and 70
- ☐ Consider survivor benefit implications
- ☐ Discuss timing as a household decision
- ☐ Verify current rules before filing

Reminder: Spousal benefits are generally based on up to 50% of the higher earner's PIA, and delayed retirement credits do not increase the spousal benefit itself. Verify current rules and estimates through SSA.gov before making a filing decision.

What this means for your household. Coordination works best when you stop thinking in terms of "my benefit" and "your benefit" and start treating Social Security as one household paycheck that needs to last through both lifetimes. Run the numbers together, even if only one of you handles the finances day to day.

Managing Age and Income Differences

Age gaps and big differences in lifetime earnings are common. They add moving parts, but they also create planning options if you handle them carefully.

Younger spouse considerations. When one spouse is several years younger, timing can be more flexible. The younger spouse has more years before reaching 62 and may have more working years ahead. A younger, lower-earning spouse may benefit from staying in the workforce longer, since additional earning years can strengthen their record and replace zeros in the 35-year calculation. Meanwhile, the older, higher-earning spouse can delay to maximize the eventual household benefit.

A common complication shows up when the older, higher earner wants to delay until 70, but the younger spouse is not yet eligible for benefits. In that gap, the household may need to lean on savings, a pension, or part-time work. The tradeoff comes later, when the higher earner's benefit (and the survivor benefit) is larger.

Higher earner delay strategies. When one spouse significantly out-earned the other, the higher earner often has the most to gain by delaying. Each year of delay between the FRA and 70 adds 8% to the higher earner's benefit. That higher number also becomes a key input for survivor benefits later.

It helps to frame this as two decisions in one. The higher earner's claiming age sets their own monthly income. It can also set the monthly income their spouse may live on after the higher earner dies.

Lower earner timing decisions. The lower-earning spouse often has a more constrained choice set. If their own PIA is well below 50% of the higher earner's PIA, they may end up receiving a spousal benefit once the higher earner files. Claiming their own smaller benefit earlier can help the household bring in income while the higher earner waits. Early-claiming reductions still apply, but the dollar impact is often smaller because the base benefit is smaller.

Even so, the lower earner should check the numbers rather than assume. If you worked part of your career and built your own record, and your own PIA is close to (or above) 50% of your spouse's PIA, your own record may be the better deal. In that case, delaying your own claim could be worth considering.

Action step: Both spouses should pull their Social Security statements from SSA.gov, compare

PIAs, identify which spouse is the higher earner, and then discuss timing options together. The gap is often smaller or larger than either spouse assumed.

Survivor Benefit Planning

Coordination is not just about monthly income today. It also affects the spouse who lives longer. Statistically, one spouse will outlive the other, sometimes by many years. When that happens, the surviving spouse does not receive two Social Security checks. They receive one: the higher of the two.

Higher earner's claiming impact. When the higher-earning spouse delays to 70 and locks in a larger benefit, that amount becomes the foundation for the survivor benefit. If the higher earner was receiving $2,900 per month at the time of death, the surviving spouse can receive up to that full amount, replacing their own smaller benefit.

Now compare that to a higher earner who filed at 62 and locked in $1,850 per month. The survivor benefit is capped at that lower amount. The surviving spouse, who may live another 10 or 15 years alone, receives $1,050 less per month for the rest of their life. Over a decade, that difference exceeds $126,000.

Survivor income protection. A surviving spouse often faces rising costs. Medical expenses tend to increase. Help around the house can become necessary. At the same time, one Social Security check disappears. If the remaining check is smaller because the higher earner filed early, the survivor may feel the squeeze during the years when flexibility is lowest.

This is the point researchers like Laurence Kotlikoff have emphasized for years: delaying the higher earner's benefit can function like built-in income protection for the surviving spouse. The claiming age effectively sets a floor for what the survivor can rely on from Social Security.

Long-term household planning. When you evaluate your claiming strategy, pressure-test it with a survivor question: if one of us dies at 80, can the surviving spouse maintain their standard of living on the remaining Social Security benefit plus whatever savings and other income are available? If the answer is uncertain, the higher earner's delay can become more valuable as an insurance-like move, even if it means a few tighter years while waiting for the larger benefit to start.

Mistake Alert and Real-Life Scenario

Mistake Alert: One of the most expensive errors couples make is having both spouses file at 62 without looking at the survivor benefit. When both file early, both benefits are permanently reduced. When the first spouse dies, the survivor receives the higher of the two reduced amounts. In many households, both spouses give up significant long-term income because neither planned for the day when only one check remains.

Before either of you files, run the numbers for the surviving spouse. Ask: What will the remaining income look like if one of us dies at 75? At 80? At 85? If the result is uncomfortable, revisit the timing.

Real-Life Scenario: John and Mary's Coordination

John is 66 with a PIA of $2,600. Mary is 63 with a PIA of $1,000. They are trying to decide when to file.

John's first instinct is to file at 66 because he is tired of working and wants to start collecting. Mary has already stopped working and wants to file now at 63. If they both file today, here is the rough result:

John at 66. John is filing one year before his FRA of 67, so his benefit is reduced by about 6.7% (5/9 of 1% per month for 12 months). His monthly check drops from $2,600 to roughly $2,427.

Mary at 63 on her own record. Mary is filing four years before her FRA of 67, so her own benefit is reduced by 25%. Her monthly check on her own record is $1,000 × 0.75 = $750.

Mary's spousal add-on. Because John has filed, Mary also qualifies for a spousal benefit on his record. The SSA calculates her total benefit in two parts: her own reduced benefit, plus a reduced spousal "differential." The differential is 50% of John's PIA minus her own PIA: $1,300 – $1,000 = $300. Because Mary is claiming 48 months before her FRA, that $300 differential is reduced by 30%, leaving $210. Mary's total monthly benefit becomes $750 + $210 = $960.

Household total: approximately $3,387 per month.

Now consider an alternative. Mary still files at 63 on her own record and collects $750. John delays until 70. At 70, his benefit grows to about $3,224 per month (his $2,600 PIA plus 24% in delayed retirement credits). Once John files, Mary's spousal differential is recalculated, but here is the rule that trips people up: **the differential is based on John's PIA**, not his actual benefit. John's delayed retirement credits do not flow through to Mary's spousal benefit. The differential is still $1,300 – $1,000 = $300, reduced the same way to $210. Mary's total still works out to about $960.

Household total after John files at 70: approximately $4,184 per month.

Spousal benefit timing errors. John and Mary's situation shows a common mistake: both spouses filing early because they want income now, without calculating the long-term cost. If John claims at 66 and dies at 80, Mary's survivor benefit would be locked at about $2,426 per month. If John delays to 70 and dies at 80, Mary's survivor benefit is about $3,224 per month. That is $798 more each month for the rest of Mary's life. Over 15 years of widowhood, that works out to more than $143,000 in additional income.

Household income optimization. The basic idea is simple: the higher earner's claiming decision affects both the household's peak income and the survivor's income floor. Couples who coordinate by having the lower earner file first and the higher earner delay often collect more total income across both lifetimes than couples who file independently.

What this means for you. If you and your spouse have different PIAs, the higher earner's delay is often the most influential decision for your household's lifetime Social Security income. Run your numbers, including what happens when only one benefit remains.

Chapter Checklist and Verification Tips

Use this checklist to confirm you have reviewed spousal benefit options and coordinated your claiming timeline.

- Pull both spouses' Social Security statements from SSA.gov
- Identify which spouse has the higher PIA
- Calculate the spousal benefit (50% of the higher earner's PIA) and compare it to the lower earner's own PIA
- Determine whether the lower earner benefits more from their own record or the spousal benefit
- Discuss whether the higher earner can delay to 70 while the household lives on other income, or the lower earner's benefit
- Calculate the survivor benefit under different claiming scenarios (higher earner at 62, FRA, and 70)
- Consider each spouse's health and life expectancy when choosing timing
- If there is a significant age gap, map out the years when each spouse becomes eligible and plan accordingly
- Verify current spousal benefit reduction percentages and rules at SSA.gov before filing
- Consider consulting a fee-only financial planner if your situation involves large income differences, age gaps, or health concerns

Verification tips:

Spousal benefit rules, reduction percentages, and delayed retirement credit rates should be confirmed at SSA.gov before making any filing decision. The basic framework (50% maximum spousal benefit, no delayed credits on spousal benefits, survivor benefit based on the deceased's actual or entitled amount) has been stable, but you should still verify current-year specifics.

If you are unsure whether your own benefit or the spousal benefit is higher, request a detailed estimate from the SSA that shows both calculations. You can do this by calling 1-800-772-1213 or visiting a local Social Security office.

Key reminders: The maximum spousal benefit is 50% of the higher earner's PIA. Spousal benefits are reduced if claimed before the FRA. Delayed retirement credits do not increase spousal benefits. The higher earner's claiming age influences both the household's peak income and the survivor's long-term income floor. Coordinating as a couple often produces better outcomes than filing independently.

Most common mistakes: Both spouses filing at 62 without considering survivor implications. Assuming spousal benefits grow with delayed retirement credits (they do not). Failing to check whether the lower earner's own benefit exceeds the spousal benefit. Making claiming decisions individually rather than as a household.

Next steps: Pull both Social Security statements. Compare PIAs. Run the survivor benefit under at least two scenarios. Decide whether the higher earner can afford to delay, then pick a coordinated timeline.

5

SURVIVOR BENEFITS: PROTECTING THE SPOUSE WHO MAY LIVE LONGER

When a spouse dies, the financial landscape shifts within days. One Social Security check stops. Household expenses rarely drop by half. The surviving spouse faces a new reality where their income has contracted while many costs remain unchanged. Survivor benefits exist specifically for this situation, and understanding how they work can mean the difference between financial stability and a slow squeeze that worsens with every passing year.

The previous chapter covered how couples can coordinate their claiming decisions to build a larger survivor benefit. This chapter focuses on what happens after a spouse dies: how survivor benefits are calculated, when you can claim them, how to switch between benefit types to maximize lifetime income, and what families with children need to know. If you are already widowed, currently planning ahead with a spouse, or helping a parent through a loss, the strategies here apply directly to your situation.

How Survivor Benefits Work

A survivor benefit allows a widow or widower to receive a Social Security payment based on the deceased spouse's earnings record. The amount depends on what the deceased was receiving (or was entitled to receive) at the time of death, along with the survivor's age when they start collecting.

Benefit calculation for survivors. The basic rule: a surviving spouse can receive up to 100% of the deceased spouse's benefit amount, including any delayed retirement credits the deceased had earned. If your spouse was receiving $2,800 per month at death, you can receive up to $2,800 per month as a survivor benefit. If your spouse had not yet filed but was entitled to a Primary Insurance Amount (PIA) of $2,400, the survivor benefit is based on that PIA. And if your spouse had earned delayed retirement credits by waiting past Full Retirement Age (FRA), those credits remain in the calculation, potentially raising your survivor benefit above the PIA.

This is a critical distinction from spousal benefits. A spousal benefit maxes out at 50% of the worker's PIA and does not include delayed retirement credits. A survivor benefit can equal 100% of what the deceased was collecting or was entitled to collect, delayed retirement credits included.

Timing restrictions and options. Widows and widowers can start collecting survivor benefits as early as age 60 (or age 50 if disabled). That is two years earlier than the minimum age for retirement benefits on your own record. However, claiming at 60 comes with a permanent reduction. The full, unreduced survivor benefit becomes available at your survivor FRA, which for most people born in 1962 or later is age 67.

If you claim at 60, the benefit is reduced to approximately 71.5% of the full survivor amount. Each month you wait between 60 and your survivor FRA, the reduction decreases. At your survivor FRA, you receive 100%.

Minimum and maximum benefits. The Social Security Administration (SSA) also provides a one-time lump-sum death payment of $255 to a surviving spouse who was living with the deceased at the time of death, or in some cases to an eligible child. The application must be filed within two years of the death. Beyond that, the minimum survivor benefit depends on the deceased's work record and benefit amount. The maximum is the full benefit the deceased was entitled to, including any delayed retirement credits earned before age 70. There is no additional growth in the survivor benefit if the deceased had already reached 70 or if the survivor waits past their own FRA to claim the survivor benefit. Once you reach your survivor FRA, you receive the full amount with no advantage to further delay of the survivor benefit itself.

Survivor Benefit Planning Worksheet

Social Security provides important protection for your surviving spouse. Use this worksheet to estimate potential survivor benefits and plan ahead.

1. Your Information

	You (Worker)	Spouse
Full Name		
Date of Birth		
Social Security Number (last 4 digits)		
Estimated Benefit at Full Retirement Age (FRA)		
Planned Claiming Age		

2. Survivor Benefit Basics (General Rules)

- A surviving spouse can receive up to 100% of the deceased spouse's benefit at the survivor's Full Retirement Age.
- If the survivor claims before Full Retirement Age, the benefit may be reduced.
- If the survivor delays past Full Retirement Age (up to age 70), the benefit may increase.
- You must have been married for at least 9 months before the worker's death (exceptions apply).

3. Estimate Your Potential Survivor Benefit

Based on Your Spouse's Record	Amount at Spouse's Full Retirement Age (FRA)	Your Estimated Survivor Benefit at Your FRA (Up to 100%)
Spouse's Estimated Benefit at FRA	$ ______	$ ______
Potential Survivor Benefit at Your FRA (Up to 100% of spouse's amount)		$ ______
If You Claim Before Your FRA (Amount May Be Reduced)		$ ______
If You Delay Past Your FRA (Up to Age 70)		$ ______

4. Questions to Discuss Before You File

- ☐ Which spouse has the higher benefit at FRA?
- ☐ Have we reviewed both of our life expectancies?
- ☐ When will we each reach our Full Retirement Age?
- ☐ Would delaying benefits increase our survivor protection?
- ☐ Do we have other income to rely on if we delay?
- ☐ If one of us passes away, will the survivor benefit be enough to meet our needs?
- ☐ Have we considered health, family history, and longevity?
- ☐ Do we understand how remarriage (if applicable) may affect survivor benefits?

Important: Actual benefits will depend on your earnings history, claiming ages, and the timing of the death. For personalized estimates, visit SSA.gov or speak with a qualified financial advisor.

Timing Strategies for Widows and Widowers

The age at which you claim a survivor benefit matters significantly. Filing early provides income sooner but locks in a permanently reduced amount. Waiting can mean a larger monthly check for the rest of your life. The right timing depends on your financial needs, your health, and whether you have your own retirement benefit that might grow larger with time.

Early survivor benefits at 60. You become eligible for a survivor benefit at age 60. At that age, the benefit is reduced to roughly 71.5% of the full survivor amount. For a deceased spouse whose full benefit was $2,400, claiming at 60 would produce approximately $1,716 per month. That is $684 less per month than waiting until survivor FRA.

Why would someone claim at 60? In many cases, financial necessity drives the decision. A widow or widower who has lost household income and has limited savings may need the cash flow immediately. Others may claim early because they plan to switch to their own retirement benefit later, a strategy covered in the next section.

FRA versus delayed claiming. Waiting until your survivor FRA gives you 100% of the deceased's benefit. Using the same example, that means $2,400 per month instead of $1,716. Over 20 years of collecting, the difference between claiming at 60 and claiming at survivor FRA exceeds $164,000 in cumulative income.

One important note: unlike your own retirement benefit, the survivor benefit does not grow past your survivor FRA. There are no delayed retirement credits on survivor benefits. Waiting from 60 to your survivor FRA eliminates the early-claiming reduction, but waiting past survivor FRA provides no further increase to the survivor amount. If the survivor benefit is your only option, there is no advantage to delaying beyond your survivor FRA.

Switching between benefit types. Here is where the timing strategy becomes powerful. Social Security rules allow you to collect one type of benefit and later switch to another. A widow or widower with their own work record has two potential benefits: the survivor benefit and their own retirement benefit. These are separate benefits with separate timing rules. You can claim one first and switch to the other later if the second benefit would be larger. This switching strategy is one of the most valuable planning tools available to surviving spouses, and it deserves a detailed look.

The Switching Strategy Explained

The switching strategy takes advantage of the fact that survivor benefits and retirement benefits are treated as two distinct benefits by the SSA. You can collect one while the other grows, then switch at the optimal time.

Survivor versus own benefit. When your spouse dies, you have a choice. You can file for the survivor benefit based on the deceased's record, or you can file for your own retirement benefit based on your own work history. If your own retirement benefit at age 70 would be larger than the survivor benefit, it makes sense to claim the survivor benefit first and switch to your own record later. If the survivor benefit is the larger of the two, you might claim your own smaller retirement benefit early and switch to the full survivor benefit at your survivor FRA.

The key principle: claim the smaller benefit first and let the larger benefit grow to its maximum before switching to it.

Optimal switching timeline. Consider a widow who is 60 years old. Her deceased husband's benefit was $2,600 per month. Her own PIA at FRA (age 67) would be $1,800, and if she delays to 70, her own benefit would grow to approximately $2,232 (with delayed retirement credits of 24%). Since $2,600 is larger than $2,232, she would benefit from claiming her own retirement benefit at 62 (reduced, but creating income) and then switching to the full survivor benefit at her survivor FRA of 67.

Now consider the reverse. A widow's deceased husband had a benefit of $1,900. Her own PIA is $2,200, and at 70, her own benefit would be approximately $2,728. In this case, she could claim the survivor benefit at 60 (receiving a reduced amount of roughly $1,358), use that income to bridge the gap, and then switch to her own retirement benefit at 70 when it reaches $2,728. She collects survivor income for 10 years while her own benefit grows to its maximum.

Maximizing lifetime income. The switching strategy works because each benefit type has different growth rules. Your own retirement benefit grows with delayed retirement credits between FRA and 70 (8% per year). The survivor benefit does not grow past your survivor FRA. By identifying which benefit will ultimately be larger at its maximum and claiming the other one first, you can collect income during the early years while preserving the larger payment for the later years when you may need it most.

This strategy requires careful calculation. The SSA will not automatically suggest it, and many widows and widowers file for the wrong benefit first because they are not aware of the option. Before you claim any benefit after a spouse's death, compare both amounts at different ages and identify the optimal switch point.

Family Benefits and Maximums

Survivor benefits extend beyond the surviving spouse. When a worker dies, certain family members may also qualify for monthly payments based on the deceased's record.

Children's survivor benefits. Unmarried children under age 18 (or under 19 if still in high school) can receive survivor benefits equal to 75% of the deceased parent's PIA. A child who became disabled before age 22 may qualify for benefits indefinitely, as long as the disability continues. These payments can provide critical support for families who lose a breadwinner while children are still at home.

A surviving spouse caring for a child under age 16 can also receive a benefit of up to 75% of the deceased's PIA, regardless of the surviving spouse's own age. This means a 45-year-old widow with young children could receive both a caretaker benefit and payments for each child, without waiting until age 60.

Family maximum limits. The SSA sets a maximum on the total amount a family can receive from one worker's record. This family maximum typically ranges from 150 to 180% of the deceased worker's PIA, depending on the PIA amount. When the combined benefits for all family members exceed the cap, each person's payment (except the surviving spouse's own retirement benefit, if claimed separately) is reduced proportionally until the total fits within the limit.

For example, if a deceased worker's PIA was $2,000, the family maximum might be about $3,500. A surviving spouse and three children could potentially qualify for benefits totaling more than $3,500, but payments would be adjusted downward so the family total does not exceed the cap.

Benefit distribution rules. The surviving spouse's benefit is calculated first, and children's benefits are then added until the family maximum is reached. As children age out of eligibility (turning 18 or finishing high school), the remaining family members' benefits may increase if they were previously reduced due to the maximum. The SSA recalculates when family composition changes.

These rules matter most for younger families. If you are a surviving spouse with dependent children, contact the SSA promptly after a spouse's death. Benefits for children can begin immediately and are often overlooked during the difficult weeks following a loss.

Mistake Alert and Real-Life Scenario

Mistake Alert: One of the most costly errors widows and widowers make is filing for the wrong benefit first and missing the switching strategy entirely. When you walk into a Social Security office after a spouse's death, the representative may process your claim for whichever benefit you ask about. If you ask for the survivor benefit when your own retirement benefit would ultimately be larger, or if you claim your own benefit when you should have taken the survivor benefit first, you may forfeit thousands of dollars in lifetime income. The SSA processes what you request. The representative is not required to analyze your optimal strategy.

Real Life Scenario: Patricia's widow benefit decision. Patricia is 62 when her husband Richard dies. Richard was receiving $2,850 per month (he had delayed until 69 before filing). Patricia's own PIA is $1,600. At 70, her own benefit would grow to approximately $1,984 with delayed retirement credits. Since the survivor benefit ($2,850 at her survivor FRA of 67) is clearly larger than her own maximum benefit ($1,984 at 70), Patricia's best strategy is to claim her own reduced retirement benefit at 62 and switch to the full survivor benefit at 67.

If Patricia files for her own benefit at 62, she receives approximately $1,120 per month (her $1,600 PIA reduced by 30% for claiming five years early). She collects that for five years. At 67, she switches to the full survivor benefit of $2,850 per month. Over those five years, she collected about $67,200 from her own benefit while preserving the larger survivor amount.

Missing optimal switching strategy. Instead, Patricia might walk into the SSA office and file for the survivor benefit at 62, thinking she should get the larger check right away. At 62, the survivor benefit is reduced to approximately $2,270 per month (the reduction phases in linearly from 71.5% at age 60 to 100% at her survivor FRA of 67). She receives that amount for the rest of her life. She never switches because the survivor benefit, even reduced, exceeds her own retirement benefit at any age.

The cost of that single decision is significant. Compare what Patricia collects under each strategy by age 87 (25 years after her husband's death):

- Filing survivor benefit at 62: $2,270 × 300 months = about $681,000
- Optimal strategy (own benefit at 62, switch to full survivor at 67): $67,200 from age 62 to 67, plus $2,850 × 240 months from 67 onward = about $751,200
- The optimal strategy produces roughly $70,000 more by age 87, and the gap widens every year Patricia lives. By age 92, the difference exceeds $105,000.

Age 60 versus FRA timing. The temptation to claim early is understandable, especially after a loss. But the math often favors waiting if you have other resources or can use the switching strategy. Before filing, calculate both benefits at multiple ages, determine which one is ultimately larger, and claim the smaller one first. A few hours of planning can be worth six figures over a lifetime.

What this means for you. If you have recently lost a spouse or are planning ahead for the possibility, remember: you likely have two separate benefits available, and the order in which you claim them matters. Take time to compare before you file. Ask the SSA to show you both your survivor benefit and your own retirement benefit at different ages.

Chapter Checklist and Verification Tips

Use this checklist to confirm you understand your survivor benefit options and have identified your optimal claiming strategy.

1. Obtain a copy of the deceased spouse's Social Security benefit information (or their most recent statement if planning ahead)
2. Compare the survivor benefit amount to your own retirement benefit at FRA and at age 70
3. Determine which benefit is ultimately larger and plan to claim the smaller one first
4. Calculate the reduction if claiming the survivor benefit before your survivor FRA

5. Consider whether the switching strategy applies to your situation
6. If you have dependent children, contact the SSA to apply for children's survivor benefits promptly
7. Check whether the family maximum applies if multiple family members will collect
8. If you plan to remarry, verify how remarriage before or after age 60 affects survivor benefit eligibility
9. Confirm current reduction percentages and survivor FRA at SSA.gov before filing

Verification tips:

Survivor benefit reduction percentages, FRA for survivors, and family maximum formulas should be verified at SSA.gov before making any filing decision. Remarriage rules are particularly important: if you remarry before age 60, you generally lose eligibility for the survivor benefit (though eligibility can be restored if the later marriage ends). Remarriage at 60 or later does not affect your survivor benefit eligibility. These rules have been stable, but always confirm the current policy.

If you are unsure which benefit to claim first, ask the SSA for a detailed comparison showing your survivor benefit and your own retirement benefit at ages 60, 62, FRA, and 70. You can request this by calling 1-800-772-1213 or visiting your local office. Consider bringing a trusted family member or a fee-only financial advisor to help you evaluate the options before signing anything.

Key reminders: The survivor benefit can equal up to 100% of the deceased's benefit, including delayed retirement credits. Survivor benefits can start as early as age 60, but early claiming reduces the amount permanently. The switching strategy allows you to collect one benefit while the other grows. The SSA processes what you request, so know your optimal strategy before you file.

Most common mistakes: Filing for the survivor benefit immediately without comparing it to your own retirement benefit at 70. Assuming you must take the survivor benefit because it seems larger right now. Failing to ask about the switching strategy. Missing children's survivor benefits after a spouse's death. Remarrying before 60 without understanding the impact on survivor eligibility.

Next steps: Pull your Social Security statement. Compare your own retirement benefit at multiple ages to the available survivor benefit. Determine which is ultimately larger. Plan to claim the smaller benefit first. If in doubt, schedule an appointment with the SSA and request both calculations in writing before filing.

6

DIVORCE AND SOCIAL SECURITY: BENEFITS YOU MAY NOT KNOW YOU CAN CLAIM

Millions of Americans who divorced years ago have no idea they may qualify for Social Security benefits based on a former spouse's work record. These benefits can apply whether or not your ex-spouse knows you are claiming them, whether or not your ex has remarried, and no matter how long ago the marriage ended. If you meet the eligibility rules, the money is yours to claim. Your ex-spouse's benefit is not reduced because you file, and the Social Security Administration (SSA) does not notify them that you applied.

For many divorced people, this comes as a relief. For some, it is the difference between a modest monthly check and one that actually moves the needle. But the rules are specific, and it pays to understand them before you file so you do not trip over an avoidable mistake.

Eligibility Requirements for Divorced Spouse Benefits

To qualify for a divorced spouse benefit, you must meet three core requirements. Each one is strict, with only limited exceptions.

The 10-year marriage requirement. Your marriage must have lasted at least 10 years. The SSA counts from the date of marriage to the date the divorce was finalized. If your marriage lasted 9 years and 11 months, you do not qualify. There is no rounding up, no exception for separations, and no workaround. What matters is the finalization date on your divorce decree.

If you are currently in divorce proceedings and your marriage is nearing the 10-year mark, the timeline matters enormously. Finalizing even one month too early can cost you decades of potential benefits.

Current marital status rules. You must be unmarried when you claim on your ex-spouse's record. If you have remarried, you generally cannot collect divorced spouse benefits from a prior marriage (remarriage rules are covered in detail later in this chapter). If your later marriage ends in divorce or by the death of that spouse, your eligibility to claim on the first ex-spouse's record may return. The SSA looks at your status on the day you apply.

You must also be at least 62 years old to file for a divorced spouse benefit, which is the same minimum age that applies to retirement and spousal claims.

Ex-spouse's benefit eligibility. Your former spouse must be entitled to Social Security retirement or disability benefits. They do not have to be collecting yet, as long as you have been divorced for at least two continuous years. That two-year rule matters. If you have been divorced for less than two years, your ex must have already filed for their own benefits before you can claim on their record. After two years have passed, you can file independently, even if your ex still has not claimed.

Your ex-spouse does not need to give permission, and their benefit amount is unaffected by your claim. Even if your ex has remarried and their current spouse is collecting spousal benefits, your divorced spouse benefit can still be paid in full if you qualify.

Divorced-Spouse Benefit Eligibility

Use this checklist to see if you may qualify for divorced-spouse benefits.

ELIGIBILITY CHECKLIST

- ☐ Marriage lasted at least 10 years
- ☐ Currently unmarried
- ☐ Age 62 or older
- ☐ Former spouse is entitled to Social Security retirement or disability benefits
- ☐ Your own retirement benefit may be lower than the possible divorced-spouse benefit
- ☐ Divorce has been final long enough, if the former spouse has not filed yet
- ☐ Claiming early may reduce the monthly amount
- ☐ Remarriage usually affects eligibility unless the later marriage ended

QUESTIONS TO REVIEW BEFORE FILING

- ☐ Have I compared my own benefit with a divorced-spouse benefit?
- ☐ Am I currently unmarried?
- ☐ Do I have the documents Social Security may ask for?
- ☐ Should I speak with Social Security before filing?

★

Social Security can confirm eligibility and benefit details based on your personal record.

What this means for you. If you were married for 10 years or longer, are currently single, and your ex-spouse has (or will have) a Social Security record, you may have a benefit available. The amount depends on your ex's Primary Insurance Amount (PIA), which is the monthly benefit they are entitled to at their Full Retirement Age (FRA).

How Divorce Affects Claiming Strategies

Divorced spouse benefits work a lot like the spousal benefits discussed in Chapter 4 on couples coordinating their claims. The big difference is that you do not need coordination. You do not have to communicate with your ex-spouse or time your decision around theirs.

Independent claiming ability. Once you have been divorced for at least two years, you can claim on your ex-spouse's record whether or not they have filed. Married spouses usually do not get that flexibility. Here, you control the timeline.

That independence can be especially helpful if your ex-spouse plans to wait until age 70 to file. A married spouse would typically need to wait for the higher earner to file before spousal benefits can be paid. If you are divorced and the two-year rule is satisfied, you are not stuck waiting.

Benefit calculation differences. The maximum divorced spouse benefit is the same as the married spousal benefit: up to 50% of your ex-spouse's PIA. If your ex has a PIA of $2,800, the maximum divorced spouse benefit at your FRA would be $1,400 per month.

Just like married spousal benefits, that amount is reduced if you claim before your own FRA. Filing at 62 with an FRA of 67 reduces the divorced spouse benefit to roughly 32.5% of your ex's PIA instead of 50%. The reduction is permanent.

The SSA also compares your own retirement benefit (based on your earnings record) with the divorced spouse benefit and pays you the higher amount. You do not get to pick between them. The calculation happens automatically. If your own PIA is $1,100 and your divorced spouse benefit would be $1,400, you would receive $1,400. If your own PIA is $1,600 and the divorced spouse benefit is $1,400, you receive $1,600 based on your own record.

Timing considerations. Divorced spouse benefits do not increase after your FRA. Delayed retirement credits do not apply to spousal or divorced spouse benefits. Waiting from 62 to FRA increases the amount, but waiting past FRA does not.

Your own retirement benefit is different. It can grow with delayed retirement credits up to age 70. That creates a sequencing question: if your own benefit at 70 would be higher than the divorced spouse benefit at FRA, you may want to think carefully about when to start each benefit. Talk with the SSA or a qualified financial planner to run the numbers for your specific situation.

Multiple Marriages and Benefit Calculations

If you have been married and divorced more than once, and more than one marriage lasted at least 10 years, you may be eligible for divorced spouse benefits tied to more than one ex-spouse. The SSA does not require you to choose a record and stick with it forever. Instead, it pays the highest benefit you qualify for.

Choosing the best ex-spouse benefit. When you file, the SSA reviews the records you may be entitled to and calculates which one pays the most. You receive the highest available amount. For example, if your first ex-spouse has a PIA of $2,200 and your second ex-spouse has a PIA of $3,000, the SSA will base your divorced spouse benefit on the $3,000 PIA because 50% of that amount is larger.

Multiple divorce scenarios. Each marriage must separately meet the 10-year requirement. A 12-year first marriage and a 7-year second marriage means you qualify based on the first marriage only. Two marriages that each lasted 10 or more years give you two potential records. The SSA can sort through this, but you should bring documentation for every qualifying marriage when you apply.

Benefit comparison methods. Before you file, request benefit estimates from the SSA that show your own retirement benefit, each divorced spouse benefit you may qualify for, and the amounts at different claiming ages. You can call 1-800-772-1213 or visit your local Social Security office to request these calculations. Seeing the numbers ahead of time makes it easier to decide when to file.

Remarriage Considerations

Remarriage can change your eligibility for divorced spouse benefits in a big way. If you understand the rules before you remarry, you can avoid unpleasant surprises later.

Benefit termination rules. If you remarry, you generally lose eligibility for divorced spouse benefits from your previous ex-spouse. The change takes effect as soon as you are legally married again. Your new marriage may create a new spousal benefit option based on your new spouse's record (once they file), but it usually closes the door on your former spouse's record.

There is an important exception. If your later marriage ends through divorce, annulment, or the death of your new spouse, your eligibility for divorced spouse benefits from a prior qualifying marriage may be restored. Again, the SSA focuses on your current marital status when you apply. If you are unmarried at that point, prior qualifying marriages can be considered.

New spouse benefits. After you remarry, your Social Security options generally shift to your new spouse's record. You may become eligible for spousal benefits based on your new spouse's PIA, under the usual rules: they must file, and you generally must be married for at least one year before claiming spousal benefits on their record. Whether your new spouse's record produces a higher or lower benefit than your ex's record depends on their earnings history.

Timing remarriage strategically. If you are considering remarriage and you are close to retirement age, run the numbers before the wedding. Compare the divorced spouse benefit you qualify for now with the spousal benefit you might receive on your new spouse's record. Sometimes the divorced spouse benefit is larger. Sometimes the new spouse's record wins.

This is personal, and it is not just about money. Still, you want to know what you are signing up for when you sign the marriage certificate, instead of learning about the financial impact after the fact.

Mistake Alert and Real-Life Scenario

Mistake Alert: One of the costliest errors divorced people make is remarrying without understanding the benefit implications. Another is never claiming divorced spouse benefits at all because they assume they no longer have any connection to their ex-spouse's Social Security record. Either mistake can cost tens of thousands of dollars over a retirement.

Real-Life Scenario: Susan's Divorced Spouse Decision

Susan was married to Daniel for 14 years before they divorced. She is now 64, has never remarried, and is considering filing for Social Security. Her own PIA based on her work history is $1,050 per month. Daniel's PIA is $2,600 per month.

If Susan files at 64 on her own record, she receives a permanently reduced benefit of about $875 per month. Because her marriage to Daniel lasted more than 10 years and they have been divorced for more than two years, she also qualifies for a divorced spouse benefit. At her FRA of 67, that benefit would be $1,300 per month (50% of Daniel's $2,600 PIA).

If Susan files at 64 and claims the divorced spouse benefit, the early-claiming reduction brings it down to about $1,083 per month. That is still higher than her own reduced benefit of $875. If she waits until 67, she receives the full $1,300.

Susan decides to wait until her FRA to maximize the divorced spouse benefit. She uses savings and part-time income to cover the gap.

Six months later, Susan begins dating someone seriously. Before accepting a marriage proposal, she checks the numbers again. Remarriage would end her access to the $1,300 divorced spouse benefit. Her new partner's PIA is $1,900, which would give her a maximum spousal benefit of $950 at FRA. Remarrying would cut her Social Security income by $350 per month compared with claiming the divorced spouse benefit.

Susan and her partner decide to talk about it directly. They weigh the financial trade-off against everything else that matters to them. Susan makes the decision knowing exactly what she would be giving up.

Documentation requirements. When you apply for divorced spouse benefits, bring your final divorce decree (showing the date of marriage and the date the divorce was finalized), your marriage certificate if you have it, your ex-spouse's Social Security number or their full name and date of birth, and your own identification documents. If you have been married more than once, bring documentation for each marriage. Missing paperwork can slow down your claim, so gather what you need well before you plan to file.

Chapter Checklist and Verification Tips

Use this checklist to confirm you have reviewed your divorced spouse benefit options:

1. Confirm your marriage lasted at least 10 continuous years (check your divorce decree for exact dates)
2. Verify your current marital status qualifies you (currently unmarried)
3. Determine whether you have been divorced for at least two years (for independent filing)
4. Request a benefit comparison from the SSA showing your own benefit versus the divorced spouse benefit
5. If you have multiple qualifying marriages, bring documentation for each and ask the SSA to compare all options
6. Understand that remarriage will end your divorced spouse benefit eligibility
7. If considering remarriage, compare the divorced spouse benefit to the potential new spousal benefit
8. Gather your divorce decree, marriage certificate, and ex-spouse's identifying information before filing

Verification tips: Confirm divorced spouse benefit rules, reduction percentages, and eligibility requirements at SSA.gov before filing. Call 1-800-772-1213 or visit a local Social Security office to request benefit calculations for your situation. Reduction factors and formulas can change, so verify the numbers that apply to your filing age and circumstances.

Key reminders: The maximum divorced spouse benefit is 50% of your ex's PIA. You must have been married for at least 10 years. You must be currently unmarried. Your ex does not need to know or approve. Remarriage generally ends your eligibility. Divorced spouse benefits do not increase after your FRA.

Most common mistakes: Failing to claim because you did not know the benefit existed. Remarrying without comparing benefit amounts. Filing too early and locking in a permanent reduction. Assuming your ex-spouse's benefit is affected by your claim (it is not).

Next steps: Pull your Social Security statement. Request a divorced spouse benefit estimate. Gather your divorce documentation. If you are considering remarriage, run the numbers first.

7

MEDICARE AND SOCIAL SECURITY: ENROLLMENT DEADLINES, COVERAGE CHOICES, AND COSTLY PENALTIES

The Social Security check you worked decades to earn can cover part of your retirement income. But if you do not have the right Medicare coverage in place at the right time, medical costs can take a startling bite out of that income every month. Medicare and Social Security decisions overlap in ways people often do not notice until it is expensive. Your enrollment timing, your coverage choices, and your understanding of penalties all affect how much of your retirement income actually stays in your pocket.

This chapter walks through each part of Medicare, explains the enrollment windows you cannot afford to miss, shows how penalties add up, and helps you coordinate Medicare with employer coverage if you are still working after age 65.

Medicare Parts A, B, C, and D Explained

Medicare is the federal health insurance program for people age 65 and older, as well as certain younger people with disabilities. It is divided into separate parts, and each one covers different types of care. Once you know what each part does, it gets easier to decide what you need and when to enroll.

Part A: Hospital Insurance

Medicare Part A covers inpatient hospital stays, skilled nursing facility care after a qualifying hospital stay, hospice care, and some home health services. Most people pay no monthly premium for Part A because they or their spouse paid Medicare taxes during their working years. If you or your spouse worked and paid Medicare taxes for at least 40 quarters (roughly 10 years), you typically qualify for premium-free Part A.

Put simply, Part A is your inpatient hospital coverage. It helps pay the bills when you are admitted to the hospital. It does not cover routine doctor visits or most outpatient procedures.

Part B: Medical Insurance

Medicare Part B covers doctor visits, outpatient care, preventive services, durable medical equipment, and many other medical services that Part A does not cover. Part B requires a monthly premium for most enrollees. The standard Part B premium changes each year. For current premium amounts, check Medicare.gov.

Here is the practical point: Part B is where most routine medical care lands. You will likely use Part B far more often than Part A. If you are already receiving Social Security benefits, the Part B premium is usually deducted directly from your Social Security check.

Part C: Medicare Advantage

Medicare Advantage plans (Part C) are offered by private insurance companies approved by Medicare. These plans include Part A and Part B coverage, and many also include prescription drug coverage. A number of Medicare Advantage plans add benefits such as dental, vision, and hearing coverage. You must have both Part A and Part B to enroll in a Medicare Advantage plan.

A good way to think about Medicare Advantage is that you are getting your Medicare benefits through a private insurer instead of directly through Original Medicare. Costs, provider networks, and rules can differ from Original Medicare. Some plans have low or even $0 premiums, but they may require you to use in-network doctors and hospitals.

Part D: Prescription Drug Coverage

Medicare Part D covers outpatient prescription drugs. If you stay with Original Medicare (Parts A and B) rather than a Medicare Advantage plan, you can add a standalone Part D plan for drug coverage. Private insurance companies offer Part D plans, and each plan has its own list of covered drugs (called a formulary), its own premiums, and its own cost-sharing structure.

If you take prescription medications regularly, Part D helps protect you from paying full retail price. Even if you take few or no medications right now, enrolling on time matters because late enrollment penalties can stick with you.

Medicare Parts A, B, C, and D

Medicare has different parts that work together to help cover your health care needs.

Medicare Part	What It Covers	Examples	How You Get It	Typical Cost
Part A Hospital Insurance	Inpatient hospital care, skilled nursing facility care, hospice care, and some home health care.	• Hospital stays • Rehab in a skilled nursing facility • Hospice care • Home health care	Usually automatic if you or your spouse have worked and paid Social Security taxes.	Most people pay $0 premium. You may pay deductibles and coinsurance.
Part B Medical Insurance	Doctor visits, outpatient care, preventive services, lab tests, X-rays, durable medical equipment, and more.	• Doctor visits • Lab tests • Outpatient surgery • Preventive care	You enroll during your Initial Enrollment Period (usually when you turn 65) or when first eligible.	Monthly premium. You may pay a deductible and coinsurance.
Part C Medicare Advantage	All Part A and Part B benefits, and often additional benefits like vision, dental, and hearing.	• All Part A & B services • Vision, dental, hearing • Wellness programs • Sometimes prescription drug coverage	You must join a private insurance plan approved by Medicare in your area (instead of Original Medicare).	Monthly premium may be $0 or more. You may pay copays and coinsurance.
Part D Prescription Drug Coverage	Prescription medications at the pharmacy.	• Generic drugs • Brand-name drugs • Many vaccines	You join a Medicare-approved prescription drug plan (available with Original Medicare or some Medicare Advantage plans).	Monthly premium. You pay deductibles, copays, and coinsurance.

Keep in mind: Costs, coverage, and plan options can vary. Review your choices every year during the Annual Enrollment Period (October 15 – December 7).

Initial Enrollment Periods and Deadlines

Medicare enrollment is not open-ended. You get specific windows to sign up, and missing them can trigger long-lasting costs. For most people, the big one is the Initial Enrollment Period (IEP).

Your 7-Month Initial Enrollment Period

Your IEP is a 7-month window centered on the month you turn 65. It begins three months before your 65th birthday month, includes your birthday month, and continues for three months after.

For example, if your birthday is in June, your IEP runs from March 1 through September 30. You have those seven months to enroll in Part A and Part B.

When you enroll during that window affects when coverage starts:

- If you enroll during the three months before your birthday month, coverage generally begins the first day of your birthday month.
- If you enroll during your birthday month, coverage typically starts the first day of the following month.
- If you enroll during the three months after your birthday month, coverage may be delayed by one to three additional months.

Bottom line: Enroll earlier in your IEP if you want coverage to start sooner. If you wait until the final months, you can end up with a gap between enrollment and the start of coverage.

Automatic Enrollment Rules

If you are already receiving Social Security benefits when you turn 65, you will generally be enrolled in Medicare Part A and Part B automatically. You should receive your Medicare card in the mail about three months before your 65th birthday.

If you are not receiving Social Security benefits at 65, you usually have to sign up for Medicare yourself. This surprises a lot of people. They assume Medicare always starts automatically, but automatic enrollment is tied to already collecting Social Security.

What This Means for You: If you delayed claiming Social Security past 65, you must take the lead on Medicare enrollment. Do not assume anyone will reach out. Mark your dates, and use Medicare.gov or your local Social Security Administration (SSA) office during your IEP.

Special Enrollment Periods

A Special Enrollment Period (SEP) lets you sign up for Medicare outside the standard windows without a penalty. The most common SEP is for people who delayed Medicare because they had health coverage through their own or their spouse's current employer.

If you are covered by a group health plan through an employer where you or your spouse is actively working, you may qualify for a SEP. This SEP allows you to enroll in Part B without penalty at any time while you are still covered by the employer plan, or within eight months of the employment ending or the coverage ending, whichever comes first.

The word to watch is "current." The coverage has to be tied to active employment. Retiree health coverage and COBRA do not qualify for a SEP.

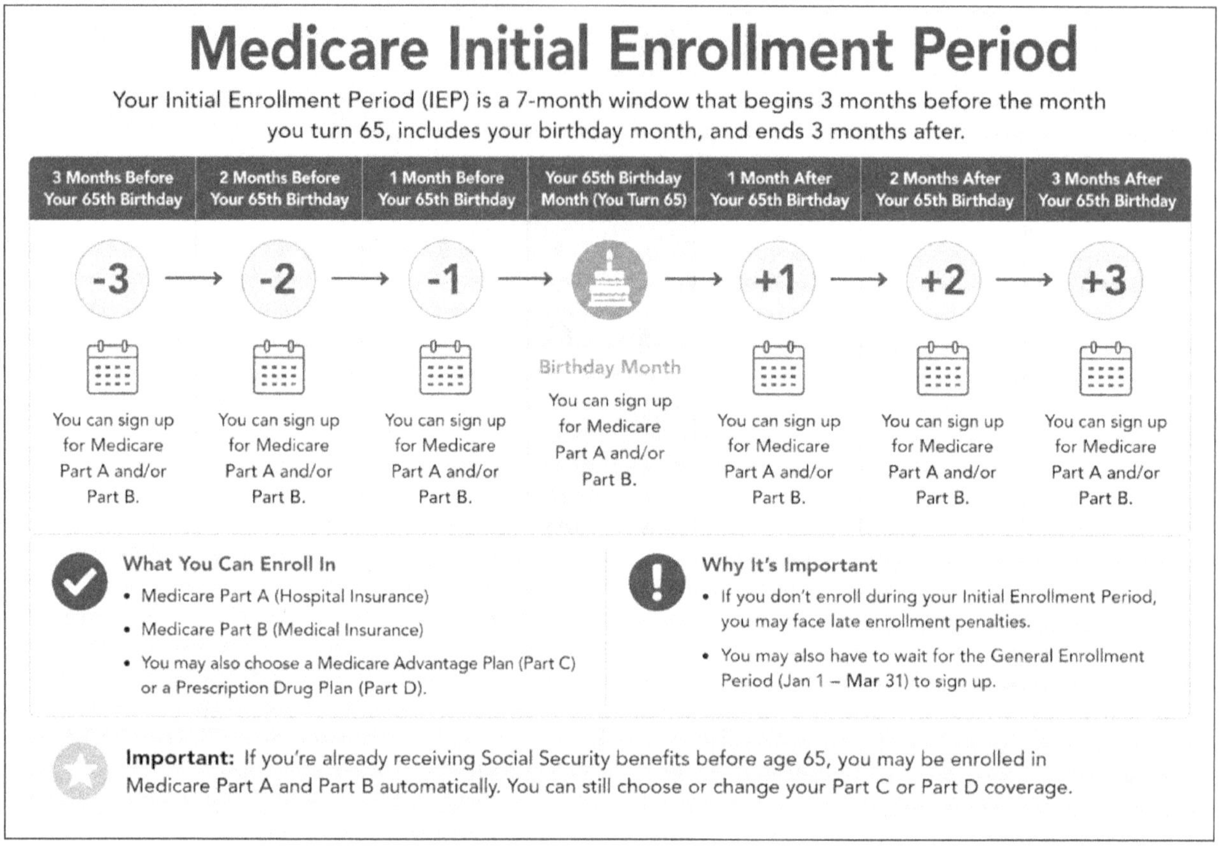

Late Enrollment Penalties and Prevention

Medicare penalties are meant to discourage people from waiting to enroll until they need care. In many cases, the penalties are permanent add-ons to your monthly premiums and last as long as you have the coverage. The best way to avoid them is to understand exactly when they apply.

Part B Late Enrollment Penalty

If you do not sign up for Part B during your IEP and you do not qualify for a SEP, you will pay a late enrollment penalty. The penalty adds 10% to your standard Part B premium for each full 12-month period you were eligible for Part B but did not enroll.

A concrete example: suppose you were eligible at 65 but did not enroll until 68. That is three full years of delay, which equals three 12-month periods. Your penalty would be 30% added to your monthly Part B premium. If the standard premium is $202.90 per month (confirm the current-year amount at Medicare.gov), a 30% penalty adds $60.87 per month. You keep paying that higher amount for as long as you have Part B.

Part D Late Enrollment Penalty

The Part D penalty is calculated differently, but it can still follow you for the long haul. **The Part D late enrollment penalty is generally 1% of the national base beneficiary premium for each**

full month you were eligible but did not have creditable coverage (including gaps of 63 days or more after your IEP). It is rounded to the nearest 10 cents, added to your premium, and recalculated each year.

For example, if you went 14 months without creditable drug coverage, your penalty would be 14% of the national base beneficiary premium added to your monthly Part D premium. The dollar amount can change each year as the base premium changes, but the penalty itself stays on your account.

Creditable Coverage: Your Protection Against Penalties

Creditable coverage is prescription drug coverage that is expected to pay, on average, at least as much as Medicare's standard Part D coverage. If you have creditable coverage through an employer, a union, or another source, you can generally enroll later without a Part D penalty.

Your current plan administrator must notify you each year whether your drug coverage is creditable. Save those letters. If Medicare asks questions later, that paperwork is often what clears things up quickly.

Mistake Alert: A lot of people assume any health insurance counts as creditable coverage for Part D. It does not. Your plan has to meet Medicare's standard for prescription drug benefits. If you are unsure, ask your plan administrator directly: "Is my prescription drug coverage creditable under Medicare Part D?" Ask for the answer in writing.

Medicare Supplement Insurance Options

Original Medicare (Parts A and B) does not cover all medical costs. You are still responsible for deductibles, copayments, and coinsurance, and those can stack up fast during a hospital stay or serious illness. Medicare Supplement Insurance, commonly called Medigap, is designed to help cover those out-of-pocket gaps.

Medigap Policy Types

Medigap policies are sold by private insurance companies and standardized by the federal government. Each plan type is identified by a letter (Plan A, Plan B, Plan C, Plan D, Plan F, Plan G, Plan K, Plan L, Plan M, and Plan N). Note that Plans C and F are no longer available to people who became eligible for Medicare on or after January 1, 2020. If you became Medicare-eligible before that date, you may still be able to enroll in them. The benefits within each lettered plan are the same, no matter which company sells it. What changes from one insurer to another is usually price and customer service, not the coverage itself.

For example, every Plan G policy covers the same benefits whether you buy it from Company X or Company Y. The monthly premium, though, can vary quite a bit.

The most popular Medigap plans tend to be Plan G and Plan N. Plan G covers nearly all out-of-pocket costs except the annual Part B deductible. Plan N often has lower premiums, but you may pay small copayments for some office visits and emergency room visits.

Guaranteed Issue Periods

Your best chance to buy Medigap is during your Medigap Open Enrollment Period. This 6-month window starts the month you are both age 65 or older and enrolled in Part B. During this period, insurance companies must sell you a Medigap policy at the standard rate, regardless of your health. They cannot deny coverage or charge you more because of pre-existing conditions.

After the window closes, insurers in most states can use medical underwriting. In plain terms, they can deny your application or charge higher premiums based on your health history.

What this means for your Medicare costs: If you want Medigap, the open enrollment window is usually when you have the most options at the best prices. If you wait, you may pay more or find that some plans are simply not available to you.

Cost Comparison Strategies

Medigap premiums can vary widely between insurance companies for the exact same plan type. Before you buy, compare premiums from at least three or four companies in your area. Also, ask how each company prices its policies:

- Community-rated (same premium for everyone regardless of age)
- Issue-age-rated (premium based on your age when you first buy)
- Attained-age-rated (premium increases as you get older)

Community-rated and issue-age-rated policies tend to be more predictable over time. Attained-age-rated policies may start lower but can climb as you age.

Note: If you choose a Medicare Advantage plan (Part C), you cannot also have a Medigap policy. Medigap works only with Original Medicare.

Coordinating Medicare with Employer Plans

If you or your spouse is still working at 65 and covered by an employer plan, Medicare gets more complicated. Which plan pays first, when you have to enroll, and how penalties apply often comes down to one detail: the size of the employer.

Working Past 65

When your employer has 20 or more employees, the employer plan is usually the primary payer, and Medicare is secondary. In that situation, you can often delay Part B without penalty, as long as you stay covered by the employer group plan through active employment.

When your employer has fewer than 20 employees, Medicare generally becomes the primary payer once you turn 65. In that case, you should enroll during your IEP even if you have employer coverage, because Medicare is expected to pay first.

So the employer size is not trivia. It determines which plan pays your bills first. Large employer (20 or more) usually gives you more flexibility with Part B timing. Small employer (fewer than 20) usually does not.

COBRA Considerations

COBRA continuation coverage does not count as coverage from a current employer for Medicare enrollment purposes. If you are on COBRA when you turn 65, or if you leave your job and elect COBRA after 65, you still need to enroll in Medicare during your IEP, or you can be hit with late penalties.

This is a common and expensive misunderstanding. People assume COBRA protects them from Medicare penalties the way active employer coverage does. It does not. For Medicare coordination, COBRA is not treated the same as coverage based on current work.

Primary Versus Secondary Coverage

When you have both Medicare and an employer plan, it matters which one is primary because that determines how claims are paid:

- Primary coverage pays first, up to its coverage limits.
- Secondary coverage may pay some or all of what is left, depending on its rules.
- If your employer plan is primary (typically because the employer has 20 or more employees and you are actively working), it pays your claims first. Medicare pays second and may cover some costs your employer plan does not.
- If Medicare is primary (typically because the employer has fewer than 20 employees), Medicare pays first. Your employer plan may then cover some remaining costs.

Once you leave your job or retire, Medicare becomes primary regardless of employer size. At that point, you have eight months to enroll in Part B through a SEP without penalty, assuming you had qualifying employer coverage tied to active employment.

Action Step: If you are approaching 65 and still working, contact your employer's benefits department and ask two questions:

1. How many employees does the company have?
2. Will the employer plan remain primary after I turn 65?

Mistake Alert and Real-Life Scenario

Real-Life Scenario Tom's Story: Still Working at 66

Tom turned 65 while still employed full-time at a company with 25 employees. His employer-sponsored health plan was excellent, so he decided to skip Medicare enrollment entirely. His HR department did not mention Medicare timing. Tom assumed his employer plan would cover everything and that he could deal with Medicare later, after he retired.

At 66, Tom retired and went to sign up for Medicare. At first, he thought he had missed his IEP and would have to wait for the General Enrollment Period, which runs from January through March each year, with coverage starting in July. Then he learned he might qualify for a Special Enrollment Period because he had been covered under a qualifying employer plan tied to active employment.

Fortunately, Tom's employer had 20 or more employees, and he had maintained group coverage through active employment the entire time. After he provided the right documentation, he qualified for the SEP and avoided the penalty. Still, the weeks of uncertainty were avoidable.

What Went Wrong

Tom's employer never explained how Medicare coordination works. He assumed it would sort itself out when he retired. He also did not keep records showing continuous employer coverage, which made the process messier than it had to be.

How to Prevent This

If you plan to work past 65, take these steps before your 65th birthday:

1. Confirm your employer has 20 or more employees.
2. Get written confirmation that your employer health plan will remain primary.
3. Ask your benefits department whether you need to enroll in Part A (many people enroll in premium-free Part A even while working since it costs nothing and can help cover certain expenses).
4. Keep every benefits enrollment letter and creditable coverage notice.
5. Mark the date you stop working. You have eight months from that date to enroll in Part B through your SEP.

Mistake Alert: If your employer has fewer than 20 employees, the rules are different. Medicare becomes primary at 65, even if you have employer coverage. In that situation, failing to enroll in Part B on time can trigger a permanent penalty. Confirm employer size and how benefits coordinate before you decide to delay anything.

Chapter Checklist and Verification Tips

Key decisions and reminders from this chapter:

1. Medicare has four parts. Part A covers inpatient hospital care. Part B covers outpatient care and doctor visits. Part C (Medicare Advantage) combines A and B through a private plan. Part D covers prescription drugs.
2. Your Initial Enrollment Period is seven months long, centered on your 65th birthday month. Missing it can lead to permanent premium penalties.
3. Part B penalties add 10% per 12-month period of delay. Part D penalties generally add 1% of the national base beneficiary premium per month without creditable coverage. Both can last as long as you have the coverage.
4. Medigap Open Enrollment is often your best window for buying supplement coverage at standard rates, with no medical underwriting.
5. Employer size determines whether your work plan or Medicare pays first.
6. COBRA coverage does not protect you from late enrollment penalties.

Verification Tips:

1. Visit Medicare.gov to confirm current Part B and Part D premiums for this year.
2. Log in to your my Social Security account at SSA.gov to see whether you are being automatically enrolled.
3. Ask your employer's benefits department for written confirmation of your plan's creditable coverage status.
4. Keep all letters from your plan administrator that mention creditable coverage.
5. If you are unsure about an enrollment deadline, call 1-800-MEDICARE (1-800-633-4227) to confirm how the rules apply to your situation.

Action Steps:

1. Mark your IEP start date on your calendar at least four months before you turn 65.
2. If you are working past 65, confirm your employer has 20 or more employees and keep documentation.
3. Compare Medigap plan premiums from at least three companies during your open enrollment window.
4. Review your prescription drug needs each year to make sure your Part D or Medicare Advantage plan still covers your medications at a reasonable cost.
5. Verify all dollar amounts, premiums, and penalty calculations against current-year figures before making enrollment decisions.

8

TAXES, IRMAA, AND THE RETIREMENT INCOME TRAPS THAT CAN SHRINK YOUR BENEFITS

A retiree named Margaret told her financial advisor she felt blindsided. She had planned carefully for Medicare enrollment, picked a Medigap plan during her open enrollment window, and started collecting Social Security at her Full Retirement Age (FRA). Then she sold a rental property in January, took a large distribution from her traditional IRA in March to pay off her mortgage, and filed her taxes the following April. The result was ugly: she owed federal income tax on 85% of her Social Security benefits, and her Medicare Part B and Part D premiums jumped by several hundred dollars per month the next year. Nobody had mentioned that one high-income year can set off consequences that show up later, long after tax season feels "done."

This chapter explains how retirement income can cause your Social Security benefits to be taxed, how certain income levels trigger Medicare premium surcharges, and what to ask before you make a major withdrawal or conversion decision.

Combined Income Thresholds for Benefit Taxation

It catches people off guard: Social Security benefits can be subject to federal income tax. Whether your benefits are taxed, and how much is taxable, depends on a figure the IRS calls "combined income," also known as "provisional income."

How Combined Income Is Calculated

Combined income equals your Adjusted Gross Income (AGI), plus any nontaxable interest (for example, interest from municipal bonds), plus one-half of your Social Security benefits. The formula looks like this:

Combined Income = AGI + Nontaxable Interest + 50% of Social Security Benefits

AGI includes income from pensions, traditional IRA and 401(k) withdrawals, wages, self-employment income, rental income, capital gains, and most other taxable sources. It does not include Roth IRA withdrawals (as long as they are qualified distributions) because those generally do not show up in AGI.

Here's the detail that trips people up: half of your Social Security gets pulled into the calculation before you even know whether it will be taxed. A modest pension, a few IRA withdrawals, and that extra 50% of Social Security can be enough to push you past the line.

The 50% and 85% Taxation Thresholds

The IRS uses two income levels to determine how much of your Social Security benefit may be taxable:

For single filers, head-of-household filers, and qualifying surviving spouses filing individually:

- Combined income between $25,000 and $34,000: up to 50% of your Social Security benefits may be taxable.
- Combined income above $34,000: up to 85% of your Social Security benefits may be taxable.

For married couples filing jointly:

- **For married couples filing jointly,** combined income between $32,000 and $44,000 makes up to 50% of benefits taxable.
- **For married couples filing jointly,** combined income above $44,000 makes up to 85% of benefits taxable.

If your combined income falls below $25,000 (single) or $32,000 (married filing jointly), your Social Security benefits are generally not subject to federal income tax.

An important note: **Social Security taxation thresholds have not been adjusted for inflation since 1983 and 1993.** Wages and retirement account balances have risen over time, but those lines have not moved. So more retirees trip over them each year, including plenty of people who would never describe themselves as "high income."

What This Means for Your Check: The tax is on your benefits, paid through your regular income tax return. **Social Security does not withhold taxes automatically unless Form W-4V is filed.** If you expect to owe tax on your benefits, you can request voluntary withholding or make quarterly estimated payments, so you are not hit with an April surprise.

State Tax Considerations

Federal tax is only part of the story. Some states also tax Social Security benefits, and the rules vary a lot. Some states exempt Social Security completely. Others tax it only above certain income levels. A few track the federal approach pretty closely.

Before you assume your benefits are state-tax-free, confirm your own state's current rules. State tax agencies update guidance, and those changes can alter your retirement budget. If you are thinking about relocating, the state treatment of Social Security is worth checking early, not after you have already moved.

Social Security Taxation Overview

Up to 85% of your Social Security benefits may be taxable, depending on your combined income.

Filing Status	Combined Income* (Provisional Income)	Amount of Benefits That May Be Taxable	How It Works	Notes
Single	$25,000 or less	Up to 0% (None taxable)	Your benefits are not taxable.	Taxes are based on your combined income, which includes adjusted gross income, non-taxable interest, and half of your Social Security benefits.
	More than $25,000 up to $34,000	Up to 50%	Up to half of your benefits may be taxable.	
	More than $34,000	Up to 85%	Up to 85% of your benefits may be taxable.	
Married Filing Jointly	$32,000 or less	Up to 0% (None taxable)	Your benefits are not taxable.	State taxes on Social Security benefits vary. Check your state's rules.
	More than $32,000 up to $44,000	Up to 50%	Up to half of your benefits may be taxable.	
	More than $44,000	Up to 85%	Up to 85% of your benefits may be taxable.	

* Combined Income (Provisional Income) = Adjusted Gross Income + Nontaxable Interest +1/2 of Social Security Benefits

Important: These are general rules. Tax laws can change. Please consult a tax professional for advice specific to your situation.

Understanding IRMAA: Hidden Medicare Surcharges

The previous chapter covered Medicare premiums, enrollment deadlines, and penalties for late enrollment. There's another cost that catches retirees off guard: **IRMAA is a surcharge added to Medicare Part B and Part D premiums based on income.**

IRMAA is not a "you messed up" penalty. It's a means-tested adjustment. Higher-income beneficiaries pay more for the same Medicare coverage. The part that stings is the timing: what you earned two years ago can decide what you pay today.

Income Thresholds for Surcharges

IRMAA thresholds are based on your Modified Adjusted Gross Income (MAGI), which, for

Medicare purposes, is your AGI plus any tax-exempt interest income. Social Security pulls that number from the tax return you filed two years before the current coverage year.

The thresholds are set in tiers. As your MAGI rises, your Part B and Part D premiums go up at each tier. The exact dollar amounts change annually, so check current-year thresholds at Medicare.gov or in the information that comes with your Social Security COLA notice.

As a general reference, the lowest IRMAA tier has often started at a MAGI just under $109,000 for single filers and $218,000 for married couples filing jointly. Higher tiers apply as income rises, with the top surcharge applying to individuals with MAGI above $500,000 (single) or $750,000 (married filing jointly). Always confirm current thresholds before you decide how much income to recognize in a given year.

Parts B and D Premium Increases

When IRMAA applies, it hits both Part B and Part D. The surcharges can be meaningful. At the lowest IRMAA tier, you might pay roughly $81.20 more per month for Part B than the standard premium. At the highest tier, the added monthly cost for Part B alone can exceed $487 per person.

Part D surcharges follow a similar tier structure. The additional monthly cost for Part D at the lowest IRMAA tier may be around $14.50, but at the highest tier, it can exceed $91 per month per person.

If both spouses are on Medicare and both are subject to IRMAA, double it. Even a mid-level tier can turn into $2,000 to $4,000 more per year than a couple expected to pay.

The Two-Year Lookback Rule

IRMAA is based on the tax return you filed two years prior. If you are paying Medicare premiums in 2026, Social Security uses your 2024 tax return (filed in 2025) to decide whether IRMAA applies. That lookback is why decisions made years ago can still change what you pay now.

Put simply: one large IRA withdrawal, a Roth conversion, a property sale, or a spike in capital gains can raise your Medicare premiums two years later. By the time the surcharge arrives, the income event may feel like old news. The bill is not.

What This Means for Your Medicare Costs: If you had a life-changing event that reduced your income significantly, such as retirement, the death of a spouse, divorce, or loss of income-producing property, you may be able to request a reduction in your IRMAA. You do this by filing Form SSA-44 with the Social Security Administration (SSA). The form asks you to document the life-changing event and provide evidence of your reduced income. If approved, SSA can use a more recent year's income instead of the two-year-old return.

IRMAA Verification Checklist

Item to Verify	What to Check	Why It Matters	Done / Notes
Medicare premium notice	Review your current Medicare premium notice to see whether an IRMAA surcharge was applied.	This confirms whether you are paying an income-related adjustment on Part B, Part D, or both.	☐ ________
Tax return year used	Verify which tax return year was used to determine IRMAA (usually the return from two years earlier).	IRMAA is generally based on older income data, not your current income.	☐ ________
Filing status	Confirm the filing status used for the determination (single, married filing jointly, married filing separately, etc.).	IRMAA thresholds depend on filing status.	☐ ________
Modified adjusted gross income (MAGI)	Check the MAGI amount from the tax return used for the IRMAA decision.	Your surcharge is based on whether your MAGI exceeds the threshold for your filing status.	☐ ________
Correct premium parts	Make sure the adjustment is applied to the correct Medicare costs.	IRMAA can affect Medicare Part B and Part D premiums.	☐ ________
Life-changing event	Consider whether a qualifying life-changing event reduced your income, such as marriage, divorce, death of a spouse, work stoppage, work reduction, loss of income-producing property, loss or reduction of pension income, or an employer settlement payment.	A qualifying event may allow you to request a new determination.	☐ ________
Support documents	Gather tax returns, SSA or Medicare notices, and documents that support any life-changing event.	You may need documentation to request a reconsideration.	☐ ________
Reconsideration request	If the determination is wrong or outdated, consider filing a reconsideration request or Form SSA-44, if appropriate.	This may reduce or remove an incorrect IRMAA surcharge.	☐ ________
Copies for your records	Keep copies of notices, forms, and all supporting paperwork.	Good records make follow-up easier if questions come up later.	☐ ________

IRMAA = Income-Related Monthly Adjustment Amount. It is an extra amount some higher-income beneficiaries pay for Medicare Part B and Part D.

Tax Planning Strategies for Retirees

Knowing how benefits are taxed and how IRMAA works is the baseline. The real question is what you can do with that information. A few planning moves can reduce taxes and help keep Medicare premiums from jumping around. There are always tradeoffs, though, and the "right" choice depends on the rest of your numbers.

Roth Conversion Timing

A Roth conversion moves money from a traditional IRA or 401(k) into a Roth IRA. You pay income tax on the amount converted in the year of the conversion, but qualified withdrawals from the Roth are generally tax-free later. Because Roth withdrawals do not count toward your AGI, they do not increase your combined income for Social Security taxation purposes, and they do not trigger IRMAA.

Timing matters. Many retirees find a window between the year they stop working and the year they begin collecting Social Security, or before age 73, when Required Minimum Distributions may begin. During that stretch, taxable income is often lower, which can make conversions less expensive from a tax-rate standpoint.

The catch is simple: every dollar you convert adds to taxable income in that year. Convert too much at once, and you can push yourself into a higher tax bracket, trigger IRMAA two years later, or cause more of your Social Security to be taxed if you are already collecting. Smaller conversions spread over several years often work out better.

Withdrawal Sequencing Strategies

The order in which you draw from different account types can change your tax picture from one year to the next. The three main account types in retirement are:

- Tax-deferred accounts (traditional IRAs, 401(k)s): withdrawals are taxed as ordinary income.
- Tax-free accounts (Roth IRAs, Roth 401(k)s): qualified withdrawals are generally not taxed and do not appear in AGI.
- Taxable accounts (brokerage accounts, savings): only gains are taxed, often at capital gains rates.

One common approach is to draw from taxable accounts first in early retirement, giving tax-deferred accounts more time to grow. Then, in lower-income years, you can consider Roth conversions or carefully sized withdrawals from traditional accounts to fill up lower tax brackets. After Required Minimum Distributions (RMDs) begin, you have less control over how much taxable income is forced onto the return.

There is no single correct sequence for everyone. The practical goal is to keep your total taxable income in a range that limits the combined effect of income taxes, Social Security benefit taxation, and IRMAA surcharges. That usually means thinking in two- to five-year blocks, not just one year at a time.

Municipal Bond Considerations

Interest from municipal bonds is generally exempt from federal income tax. That is why some retirees use municipal bonds to generate income without increasing their federal tax bill.

But there's a detail people miss: tax-exempt interest from municipal bonds is included in the combined income formula that determines whether your Social Security benefits are taxed. It also counts toward MAGI for IRMAA purposes. So while municipal bond interest may not raise your federal income tax directly, it can still push you over the thresholds that increase Social Security taxation or Medicare premiums.

This does not make municipal bonds a bad choice. It just means the interest needs to be part of the calculation when you estimate your combined income and MAGI for the year.

Managing Retirement Account Withdrawals

Retirement withdrawals affect more than your checking account balance. Each decision can create tax ripple effects, including how much of your Social Security is taxed and whether IRMAA shows up on your Medicare premiums.

Traditional Versus Roth Strategies

Traditional IRA and 401(k) withdrawals are taxed as ordinary income. Every dollar you take from a traditional account adds to your AGI, increases your combined income, and counts toward your MAGI for IRMAA.

Roth IRA withdrawals, when qualified, do not add to AGI. They do not count toward combined income for Social Security taxation. They do not affect IRMAA calculations. That makes Roth accounts especially useful in years when you need extra cash but want to stay below key thresholds.

If you have both traditional and Roth accounts, you have options. In a year when income is already high (maybe a pension, part-time work, or an RMD), pulling extra money from a Roth can keep you from piling on more taxable income. In a year when income is unusually low, you might do the opposite: take more from traditional accounts or convert some funds while you are still in a lower bracket.

Required Minimum Distributions

Once you reach the RMD age (73 if you were born between 1951 and 1959; 75 if you were born in 1960 or later, under current law, verify at IRS.gov), you must begin taking minimum withdrawals from traditional IRAs and most employer retirement plans each year. You cannot keep money in tax-deferred accounts forever.

RMDs are calculated based on your account balance and life expectancy tables published by the IRS. The larger your traditional balances, the larger your RMDs tend to be. Large RMDs can push you into higher tax brackets, trigger or increase IRMAA, and cause more of your Social Security to be taxed.

That is one reason some retirees look at Roth conversions in the years before RMDs begin. By shrinking the traditional balance through planned conversions, you can reduce future RMDs and the tax issues that come with them.

Tax Bracket Management

Each year, you have a certain amount of room left in your current tax bracket before the next bracket kicks in. Managing brackets simply means knowing where you are and planning withdrawals so you stay within a bracket you are comfortable with, when possible.

For example, if your taxable income from pensions, Social Security, and other sources leaves you $15,000 below the top of the 22% bracket, you could potentially withdraw up to $15,000 from a traditional IRA and still stay within that bracket. Go a little higher, and you may push some income into the 24% bracket.

The same idea applies to IRMAA thresholds. If your income is sitting near a tier cutoff, a few thousand dollars recognized in the wrong year can translate into hundreds more per month in Medicare surcharges for the entire year.

Action Step: Before making large withdrawals, estimate your full-year income from all sources. Start with last year's return, adjust for known changes, then check where you land relative to bracket edges, Social Security taxation thresholds, and IRMAA tiers. If you are close to a cutoff, consider splitting withdrawals across two calendar years.

Mistake Alert and Real-Life Scenario

Real-Life Scenario David's Story: One Large IRA Withdrawal, Two Years of Consequences

David retired at 66 and began collecting Social Security. His monthly benefit was $2,400. He had a traditional IRA worth about $480,000 and a small pension that paid $1,200 per month. In his first year of retirement, he withdrew $120,000 from his IRA to pay off his remaining mortgage balance. He wanted to be debt-free heading into his 70s.

He took the withdrawal as a lump sum in October. When tax season arrived, the consequences piled up:

His combined income for the year was well above $44,000 (married filing jointly), which meant 85% of his Social Security benefits were taxable. His federal income tax bill was much higher than expected because the $120,000 IRA withdrawal pushed him from the 22% bracket into the 32% bracket on a portion of the withdrawal.

Then, two years later, David received a notice that his Medicare Part B premium would increase substantially. His MAGI from the withdrawal year triggered the second IRMAA tier. His wife, who was also on Medicare, received the same notice. Together, they paid approximately $3,600 more in Medicare premiums that year than they would have at the standard rate.

What Went Wrong

David chased one goal, eliminating the mortgage, without looking at how the withdrawal would collide with Social Security taxation, federal tax brackets, and IRMAA two years later. He didn't spread the withdrawal over multiple years, and he didn't run the plan past a tax professional before pulling the trigger.

How to Prevent This

If you are considering a large withdrawal from a traditional retirement account, ask these questions first:

1. What will my total taxable income be this year if I add this withdrawal?
2. Will this push my combined income above the Social Security taxation thresholds?
3. Will this push my MAGI above an IRMAA tier two years from now?
4. Could I spread this withdrawal over two or three years to stay in a lower bracket?
5. Should I consult a tax professional or financial advisor before making this decision?

Mistake Alert: One high-income year does not just affect one tax return. It can trigger higher Medicare premiums for an entire year, two years later. It can also shift your Social Security taxation from 50% to 85% of benefits in the withdrawal year. Model the full chain reaction before you make a big move with traditional retirement accounts.

Chapter Checklist and Verification Tips

Key reminders from this chapter:

- Up to 85% of your Social Security benefits may be subject to federal income tax depending on your combined income.
- Combined income includes your AGI plus nontaxable interest plus half your Social Security benefits.
- IRMAA surcharges increase your Medicare Part B and Part D premiums based on income from the two years prior.
- Large IRA withdrawals, Roth conversions, property sales, and capital gains can all trigger IRMAA and increased Social Security taxation.
- Roth IRA withdrawals generally do not count toward combined income or MAGI.
- Municipal bond interest, while federally tax-exempt, still counts in the combined income formula.

Verification Tips:

- Check current IRMAA thresholds at Medicare.gov or in your annual Social Security COLA notice before making withdrawal decisions.
- Review your most recent tax return to see your current AGI and MAGI and estimate where you fall relative to the taxation and IRMAA thresholds.
- Plan withdrawal timing across multiple years rather than taking one large distribution.
- Consider working with a tax professional or financial advisor before executing Roth conversions, large IRA withdrawals, or property sales. The cost of professional advice is often far less than the cost of triggering an avoidable IRMAA surcharge or a higher tax bracket.
- Verify current tax bracket boundaries, IRMAA tiers, and Social Security taxation thresholds at IRS.gov and Medicare.gov each year, as these figures may be adjusted annually.

9

SPECIAL SITUATIONS: PUBLIC PENSIONS, SELF-EMPLOYMENT, MILITARY SERVICE, DISABILITY, AND FOREIGN WORK

Most Social Security rules apply the same way to everyone. Your benefit is based on 35 years of earnings, adjusted for inflation, run through a progressive formula, and paid starting at the age you claim. But some work histories change how those rules land. If you worked for a state or local government, ran your own business, served in the military, received disability benefits, or earned income in another country, extra provisions can affect how much you receive.

These provisions exist because Social Security was built around a fairly standard private-sector career. People who fall outside that model can end up with different rules for credits, benefit calculations, or how Social Security coordinates with other programs. The problem is that the "special" rules are often the ones that shrink your expected benefit, change your filing strategy, or make your Social Security statement look better than reality.

This chapter covers the five most common special situations. For each one, you will see how it connects to Social Security, what to double-check, and what to ask before you file.

Public Pensions and Social Security Coordination

If you spent part of your career working for a federal, state, or local government that did not participate in Social Security, retirement used to come with an extra layer of complexity. Many teachers, firefighters, police officers, postal workers, and other government employees earned pensions from jobs where Social Security taxes were never withheld. For decades, two provisions reduced what these workers received from Social Security: the Windfall Elimination Provision (WEP) and the Government Pension Offset (GPO). The Social Security Fairness Act repealed both, signed into law on January 5, 2025, for benefits payable after December 2023. The sections below explain how those provisions worked, why they mattered, and what the repeal means for affected retirees today.

The Windfall Elimination Provision (WEP). Until January 2024, WEP reduced your own Social Security retirement benefit if you received a pension from employment where you did not pay Social Security taxes. The Social Security Fairness Act, signed into law on January 5, 2025, repealed WEP for monthly benefits payable after December 2023. As explained in Chapter 1, your Primary Insurance Amount (PIA) is normally calculated using a formula that replaces 90% of the first portion of your Average Indexed Monthly Earnings (AIME). Under the old WEP rules, the 90% factor was reduced for workers who had fewer than 30 years of "substantial earnings" covered by Social Security.

In plain English: if you worked 20 years for a school district that did not pay into Social Security, and you also worked 15 years in private-sector jobs that did, WEP could lower your Social Security check. The size of the cut depended on how many years of substantial covered earnings you had. For benefits payable after December 2023, this reduction no longer applies, and many retirees who were previously subject to WEP have seen their full benefit restored.

The Government Pension Offset (GPO). GPO affected spousal and survivor benefits for people who received a government pension from non-covered employment. Before its repeal, the offset reduced the spousal or survivor benefit by two-thirds of the non-covered pension amount, and for some people, it wiped out the spousal or survivor benefit entirely. The same Social Security Fairness Act that repealed WEP also repealed GPO, effective for benefits payable after December 2023. If you previously chose not to apply for spousal or survivor benefits because GPO would have eliminated them, you may now want to apply.

Recent legislative changes. Congress had debated repeal for decades before passing the Social Security Fairness Act in late 2024. The SSA began recalculating affected benefits in February 2025, with retroactive payments back to January 2024. Most affected beneficiaries did not need to take action because the adjustment was automatic. If you previously did not apply for spousal or survivor benefits because GPO would have eliminated them, you may want to apply now. Verify your specific situation at SSA.gov.

What this means for your check: If you have a government pension from non-covered work and your benefit was previously reduced by WEP or GPO, the SSA has been automatically recalculating affected benefits since February 2025. Pull a fresh Social Security statement from your my Social Security account to see your current, unreduced benefit. If you previously did not apply for spousal or survivor benefits because GPO would have eliminated them, contact the SSA to discuss applying now.

Planning strategies for dual-pension retirees. If you have both a government pension and Social Security eligibility, take these steps:

- If you previously did not apply for spousal or survivor benefits because GPO would have eliminated them, contact the SSA to discuss applying now that GPO has been repealed.
- Keep documentation of all pension sources and covered-employment years.

- As covered in Chapter 8, your government pension income also counts toward your combined income for Social Security taxation purposes and your Modified Adjusted Gross Income (MAGI) for Income-Related Monthly Adjustment Amount (IRMAA) calculations. A government pension paired with Social Security can push you over the thresholds where benefits become taxable, or Medicare premiums rise.

Self-Employment and Social Security Credits

With a traditional employer, Social Security taxes are split between you and the company. Each side pays 6.2% for Social Security and 1.45% for Medicare. When you work for yourself, you cover both halves. That is the Self-Employment Contributions Act (SECA) tax.

SECA tax obligations. As a self-employed worker, you owe 12.4% for Social Security and 2.9% for Medicare on your net self-employment income, for a combined rate of 15.3%. You can deduct half of this amount when calculating your Adjusted Gross Income (AGI), which helps. Still, the full amount counts when it comes to earning Social Security credits and building your benefit.

The Social Security portion of SECA applies only up to the annual maximum taxable earnings limit, which changes each year. Check the current limit at SSA.gov. Income above that cap is still subject to the 2.9% Medicare tax, but it does not increase your Social Security benefit.

Credit accumulation rules. You earn Social Security credits based on net income. In 2026, you need $1,890 in net earnings to earn one credit (the amount adjusts annually with inflation; verify at SSA.gov). You can earn a maximum of four credits per year, and you need 40 credits (roughly 10 years of work) to qualify for retirement benefits.

For self-employed workers, net profit is what matters. Gross revenue does not count for credit purposes. If your business brings in $80,000 but your net profit after deductions is $4,000, you earn credits based on the $4,000.

Net profit calculations and your benefit. Your Social Security benefit calculation, as described in Chapter 1, uses your highest 35 years of earnings. For self-employed workers, the earnings that go into that calculation are your net self-employment income (after the SECA deduction adjustment). If you have years of low net profit because of heavy business deductions, those lower-earning years can end up in your top 35 and pull down your AIME.

One way to frame it: aggressive tax deductions can lower your tax bill now, but they also lower the earnings that get credited to your Social Security record. Reporting $20,000 in net profit instead of $60,000 (because of legitimate deductions) means your future benefit is being built on the smaller number. Over a long career, that difference can show up as a smaller monthly check.

What this means for your check: There is a real tradeoff between minimizing self-employment taxes today and building higher Social Security income later. You do not have to choose an extreme, but you should know what you are trading when you decide how much profit to report.

Action Step: Review your Social Security statement at SSA.gov and compare the earnings shown for self-employment years against your Schedule SE filings. If you see discrepancies, gather your tax returns and contact the Social Security Administration (SSA) to correct the record, as outlined in Chapter 1's discussion of common errors.

Military Service and Disability Transitions

Military service credits. If you served in the United States military, your time in service counts toward Social Security. Active-duty military pay has been covered by Social Security since 1957. For earlier service, special wage credits may apply for service between 1940 and 1956.

For service from 1957 through 1977, military members received additional deemed wage credits of $300 per quarter. From 1978 through 2001, credits were $100 for every $300 in basic pay, up to $1,200 annually. These credits were added to your earnings record to account for in-kind compensation such as housing and food allowances. They were added automatically by the Department of Defense and should appear on your Social Security statement. For service in 2002 and later, military pay is reported as regular wages. Either way, verify that all years of service show up correctly on your Social Security earnings record.

VA disability coordination. Veterans Affairs (VA) disability compensation and Social Security benefits are separate programs with different eligibility rules. You can receive VA disability payments and Social Security retirement benefits at the same time. One does not reduce the other. VA disability is tax-free, and it does not count toward your combined income for Social Security taxation purposes or your MAGI for IRMAA.

Social Security Disability Insurance (SSDI) and VA disability can also be received at the same time. If you qualify for both, each program pays based on its own criteria. A VA rating and an SSDI determination are separate decisions.

Coordination matters in one practical spot: if you are receiving VA disability and you apply for SSDI, the SSA may use your military medical records as part of the SSDI evaluation. Having your VA documentation organized can speed up the SSDI application process.

SSDI to retirement transitions. If you are currently receiving SSDI benefits, your payments automatically convert to Social Security retirement benefits when you reach your Full Retirement Age (FRA). The amount stays the same, and you do not file a new application. The SSA handles the conversion.

One detail to know: SSDI benefits are calculated as if you claimed at your FRA. When the conversion happens, your retirement benefit equals your PIA. You cannot earn delayed retirement credits while you are on SSDI. If your health improves and you return to substantial work before FRA, SSDI payments would stop. At that point, you could potentially earn delayed credits by waiting past the FRA to claim retirement benefits.

Medicare timing is affected, too. SSDI recipients qualify for Medicare after 24 months of disability payments, regardless of age. When you transition from SSDI to retirement benefits at FRA, your Medicare coverage continues without interruption.

International Considerations and Foreign Work

If you worked outside the United States or you live abroad while collecting Social Security, a different set of rules determines how foreign employment and residence affect your benefits.

Totalization agreements. The United States has bilateral Social Security agreements, called totalization agreements, with about 30 countries. These agreements do two things: they help prevent you from paying Social Security taxes to both countries on the same work, and they let you combine work credits from both countries to meet eligibility requirements.

For example, if you worked 7 years in the U.S. and 5 years in Germany, you might not have enough credits to qualify in either country by itself. Under the totalization agreement, you can combine those years to meet the 10-year (40-credit) minimum for U.S. benefits. Your U.S. benefit would still be calculated using only your U.S. earnings, but the foreign credits can help you qualify.

Each agreement is different, and the details depend on the country involved. The SSA maintains a list of current agreements at SSA.gov.

Foreign pension coordination. Foreign pensions historically interacted with WEP in the same way as U.S. government pensions from non-covered employment, since the key question was whether Social Security taxes had been paid on that work. With WEP repealed for benefits payable after December 2023, a foreign pension from non-covered work no longer reduces your U.S. Social Security benefit. Confirm your specific situation at SSA.gov, especially if your foreign work was in a country with a totalization agreement.

Resident versus non-resident rules. U.S. citizens can generally receive Social Security payments while living abroad in most countries. There are a few exceptions, including countries where the U.S. Treasury cannot send payments. Non-citizens face more restrictions. If you are a non-citizen living outside the U.S., eligibility depends on your citizenship, your country of residence, and how long you have been outside the country.

The SSA applies an "alien nonpayment provision" that can stop benefits for non-citizens who have been outside the U.S. for more than six consecutive months, unless an exception applies. Exceptions exist for citizens of countries with totalization agreements and for other qualifying cases.

What this means for your check: If you plan to retire abroad, confirm your payment eligibility before you move. Use the SSA's payment abroad screening tool at SSA.gov. If you earned income in another country, verify whether a totalization agreement applies to help you qualify for benefits.

Mistake Alert and Real-Life Scenario

Real-Life Scenario: Teacher Linda Navigates Pension Coordination

Linda taught high school English for 22 years in a state where teachers did not pay into Social Security. Earlier in her career, she worked 12 years in private-sector publishing, earning Social Security credits during that time. When she checked her Social Security statement online, it showed an estimated monthly benefit of $1,100 at her FRA of 67.

She assumed she would receive both her teacher's pension of $2,800 per month and the full $1,100 from Social Security. She was wrong.

If Linda had retired before January 2024, WEP would have applied to her Social Security benefit. With only 12 years of substantial covered earnings, the WEP reduction would have brought her Social Security payment down to about $680 per month, or $420 less than her statement indicated. Under current law, with WEP repealed by the Social Security Fairness Act, Linda receives the full $1,100 per month.

Linda also expected to claim a spousal benefit based on her husband's record after he filed. Before its repeal, GPO would have reduced her potential spousal benefit by two-thirds of her teacher's pension. Two-thirds of $2,800 is about $1,867, and since the spousal benefit would have been roughly $1,050, GPO would have eliminated it entirely. Under current law, with GPO repealed, Linda is eligible for the full spousal benefit once her husband files.

Under the old rules, Linda's retirement income would have been nearly $17,500 per year less than she had planned for (about $5,000 from the WEP reduction to her own benefit and roughly $12,600 from the GPO elimination of her spousal benefit). The repeal of WEP and GPO restores that income for Linda and millions of other public-sector retirees in similar situations.

Mistake Alert: Older Social Security statements (issued before February 2025, when the SSA began the WEP/GPO recalculation) may reflect outdated WEP-reduced estimates. If you have a pension from employment where Social Security taxes were not withheld, pull a fresh statement from your my Social Security account to see your current, unreduced benefit. Confirm that any prior reduction has been removed from your benefit calculation.

Government employees caught off-guard. Linda's situation was common among teachers, police officers, firefighters, postal workers, and federal civilian employees hired before January 1, 1984 (most of whom remained under the non-covered CSRS system rather than the Social Security-covered FERS system that replaced it). Many workers in these roles discovered the WEP/GPO impact only when they applied for benefits, which was usually too late to adjust their plans. With the repeal of both provisions, these workers now receive their full Social Security benefit alongside their pension.

Planning around public pension rules. If you are in a similar situation, verify that any prior WEP or GPO adjustments have been removed from your benefit. The SSA has been recalculating affected benefits automatically since February 2025, but if your benefit doesn't reflect the change, contact the SSA. If you previously chose not to apply for spousal or survivor benefits because GPO would have eliminated them, this is a strong time to revisit that decision.

Chapter Checklist and Verification Tips

Self-Employment, Public Pension, Military, Disabilit and Foreign Work Considerations

Use this quick-reference table to identify special situations, understand how they may affect benefits, and verify the key steps before you file.

Special Situation	Relevant Provision / Rule	Potential Impact on Benefits or Planning	Verification Step
Public pension from non-covered government work	WEP and GPO were repealed by the Social Security Fairness Act	Older estimates may still show outdated reductions. Pension income can still affect taxes and IRMAA.	Pull a fresh SSA statement and confirm any old WEP/GPO reduction has been removed.
Self-employment income	SECA tax; credits based on net earnings	Net profit affects Social Security credits and future benefit amount. Large deductions may lower future benefits.	Compare SSA earnings record with Schedule SE / tax returns for self-employment years.
Military service	Military wages count toward Social Security; older service may include deemed wage credits	Missing service years or credits can reduce your recorded earnings history.	Review your earnings record and confirm all service years appear correctly.
VA disability compensation	Separate from Social Security retirement and SSDI	VA disability generally does not reduce Social Security retirement benefits and is generally tax-free.	Keep VA records organized, especially if applying for SSDI.
SSDI to retirement transition	Automatic conversion at Full Retirement Age (FRA)	Retirement benefit usually replaces SSDI automatically at the same amount; Medicare generally continues.	Confirm your expected FRA transition timing and Medicare continuation.
Foreign work	Totalization agreements may apply	Foreign work credits may help you qualify, but U.S. benefits are still based on U.S. earnings.	Check whether a totalization agreement applies to the country involved.
Living abroad while collecting benefits	Payment eligibility depends on citizenship, residence, and SSA rules	Some beneficiaries can receive payments abroad, but restrictions may apply.	Use SSA's payment-abroad screening tool and confirm eligibility before moving.

Verification Checklist

- ☐ Confirm whether your pension came from covered or non-covered employment
- ☐ Review your Social Security earnings record for self-employment years
- ☐ Verify military service years and any special credits
- ☐ If receiving SSDI, confirm your FRA conversion timeline
- ☐ Check whether foreign work qualifies under a totalization agreement
- ☐ Confirm payment eligibility if you plan to retire abroad
- ☐ Verify current rules at SSA.gov before making a filing decision

Reminder: Special situations often create the biggest surprises in Social Security planning. Public pensions, self-employment, military service, disability status, and foreign work can all change what you should verify before filing.

1. Confirm whether your government pension is from covered or non-covered employment
2. Confirm that any prior WEP or GPO reductions have been removed from your benefit (the SSA has been recalculating these automatically since February 2025)
3. Review your Social Security earnings record for all self-employment years
4. Verify that military service years and any deemed wage credits appear on your record
5. If receiving SSDI, confirm your expected transition date and Medicare continuation
6. Check whether a totalization agreement applies to any foreign work you performed
7. Confirm payment eligibility if you plan to live outside the U.S. during retirement
8. Document all pension sources, both domestic and foreign, and bring this information to any meeting with the SSA
9. Verify the current status of WEP, GPO, and the Social Security Fairness Act at SSA.gov, as future legislation may further change these rules

Key reminders: The Social Security Fairness Act repealed WEP and GPO for benefits payable after December 2023, restoring full Social Security benefits for public-sector workers with pensions from non-covered employment. Self-employment income builds your benefit based on net profit after deductions. Military service counts toward Social Security credits. SSDI converts to retirement benefits automatically at FRA. Totalization agreements can help you qualify if you split your career between the U.S. and another country.

Most common mistakes: Working with an outdated Social Security statement that still reflects a WEP reduction (pull a fresh one). Failing to apply for spousal or survivor benefits after the repeal of GPO. Minimizing self-employment taxes without understanding the long-term benefit impact. Failing to verify military wage credits on your earnings record. Assuming foreign work does not interact with U.S. benefits.

Next steps: Identify which special situations apply to you. Use the SSA's online calculators to get adjusted estimates. Gather documentation of all pension sources and employment history. Contact the SSA with questions specific to your situation before you file.

10

BEFORE YOU FILE: DOCUMENTS, DEADLINES, ACCOUNTS, AND FINAL CHECKS

The claiming decision gets most of the attention: when to file, which benefit to claim, and how much you will receive. But the filing process has its own requirements, and those can delay benefits, create confusion, or cause you to miss a planned start date. This chapter walks you through what to do before you submit your application, from setting up your online account to gathering the right paperwork to knowing what happens after you hit "submit."

Think of this chapter as a pre-flight checklist. Every item is here because real applicants have been tripped up by missing documents, expired identification, or simple misunderstandings about how the Social Security Administration (SSA) processes claims. Completing these steps early can save you weeks of back-and-forth and helps keep your first payment on the timeline you planned for.

Setting Up Your my Social Security Account

Your first step, ideally months before you plan to file, is creating a my Social Security account at SSA.gov. This free online account is the main tool for managing your relationship with the SSA, both before and after you begin receiving benefits.

What the account lets you do. A my Social Security account lets you view your earnings history year by year, check estimated benefits at age 62, Full Retirement Age (FRA), and 70, request a replacement Social Security card, check the status of a pending application, change your address or direct deposit information after benefits begin, and download official benefit verification letters. Before you file, the most important task is reviewing your earnings record for accuracy. Errors in your earnings history can lower your benefit because they feed directly into the calculation.

The creation process. Visit SSA.gov and select "Sign in / Create an Account." You will be directed to create a Login.gov or ID.me account, which handles identity verification for federal websites. You will need a valid email address, a phone number that can receive text messages or calls, and either a state-issued ID or a passport for the identity-verification step.

Identity verification requirements. The SSA uses Login.gov or ID.me to confirm your identity. With Login.gov, you may need to upload a photo of your driver's license or state ID and take a selfie for a facial match. With ID.me, you may be able to verify through a video call with a representative if the automated process fails. For straightforward cases, verification often takes 5 to 15 minutes. Delays are more likely if your photo ID is expired or your name does not match SSA records exactly.

Mistake Alert: If your current legal name does not match what the SSA has on file, your account setup may fail. This is common for people who changed their name through marriage or divorce but never updated their records with the SSA. If this happens, you will need to visit a local Social Security office with your name-change documents (marriage certificate, divorce decree, or court order) and your updated ID before you can complete the online setup.

What this means for your timeline: Do not wait until the week you plan to file to create this account. Give yourself at least two to three months of lead time. If you run into verification problems, you will have time to fix them without pushing back your filing date. Once your account is active, log in and review your earnings record carefully. Compare it against your tax records or W-2 forms. Report discrepancies to the SSA right away. Corrections can take several weeks.

Required Documents for Application

When you apply for Social Security retirement benefits, the SSA needs to verify your identity, age, citizenship, and sometimes your marital and work history. Having these documents ready before you start the application helps prevent delays and lowers the odds that the SSA will come back later asking for more information.

Birth certificate. You will need your original birth certificate or a certified copy issued by the state where you were born. Confirm current SSA requirements at SSA.gov, because hospital-issued certificates are typically not accepted. In most cases, the SSA wants certified copies from a vital records office. If you were born outside the United States, you will need your foreign birth certificate and, depending on your citizenship status, additional documentation such as a Certificate of Naturalization or a valid U.S. passport.

If you cannot locate your birth certificate, contact the vital records office in the state where you were born. Most states let you order certified copies online or by mail, but processing times range from a few days to several weeks.

Proof of citizenship or lawful status. For U.S. citizens born in the United States, a birth certificate typically satisfies this requirement. For naturalized citizens, the Certificate of Naturalization (Form N-550 or N-570) or a U.S. passport works. Non-citizens applying for benefits will need current immigration documents, such as a Permanent Resident Card (green card) or an I-94 Arrival/Departure Record.

Military discharge papers. If you served in the U.S. military before 1968, provide your DD-214 (Certificate of Release or Discharge from Active Duty). Military service after 1968 is usually recorded in the SSA system through payroll reporting, but having your DD-214 available can still help resolve discrepancies.

Tax returns and W-2 forms. Bring your most recent tax return and your W-2 or 1099 forms for the current and previous year, especially if you are still working or were recently employed. If you are self-employed, bring your most recent Schedule SE and Schedule C. These documents help the SSA verify recent earnings that may not yet show up in its system. It can take more than a year for current-year earnings to appear in an SSA earnings record.

Marriage and divorce documentation. If you are applying for spousal benefits, bring your marriage certificate. If you are applying based on an ex-spouse's record, bring both the marriage certificate and the divorce decree. Widows and widowers should bring the deceased spouse's death certificate along with the marriage certificate.

Bank information for direct deposit. The SSA strongly encourages direct deposit. Bring a voided check or a bank statement showing your account number and routing number. If you prefer to receive benefits on a Direct Express debit card, you can request that option during the application process.

What this means for your timeline: Start gathering documents at least 60 to 90 days before your intended filing date. Some documents, like birth certificates from other states or countries, can take weeks to arrive. Missing even one required document can put your application on hold.

The Ultimate Before-You-File Master Checklist

Filing for Social Security affects your monthly income for the rest of your life. Before you submit your application, make sure each part of your plan is actually in place. This master checklist pulls together the decisions, verifications, and prep work from earlier chapters into one final review.

Decision confirmation steps:

- Confirm your planned filing age. Review whether you are claiming at 62, FRA, 70, or somewhere in between, and make sure you understand the permanent reduction or increase tied to that age. Recheck the comparison you made in earlier chapters.

- Verify your benefit estimate. Log in to your my Social Security account and confirm the estimated monthly amount at your planned claiming age. If your statement was generated before February 2025 and you have a pension from non-covered employment, the older estimate may reflect a WEP reduction that no longer applies. Pull a fresh statement to see your current, unreduced benefit.
- Confirm your FRA. Your Full Retirement Age depends on your birth year. For people born between 1943 and 1954, Full Retirement Age is 66. For those born between 1955 and 1959, it increases by two months for each year. For people born in 1960 or later, Full Retirement Age is 67. Verify your specific FRA because filing even one month early results in a permanent reduction.

Timeline verification steps:

- Check your desired benefit start date. Social Security benefits are paid in the month they are due, and your payment date is based on your birthday. Payments arrive on the second, third, or fourth Wednesday of the month, depending on whether you were born on the 1st through 10th, 11th through 20th, or 21st through 31st. If you want your first payment to arrive in January, you should file well ahead of time to allow for processing. Also, note the difference between your filing date and your benefit start date. If your first payment is scheduled for January, your benefit start date would be December, so you would need to file at least one month before December. The SSA recommends applying up to four months before you want benefits to begin.
- Verify the earnings test if you are still working. If you will be under FRA for any part of the year you file, and you expect to earn above the annual earnings limit, part of your benefits may be temporarily withheld. Check the current-year earnings limit at SSA.gov before you file.
- Confirm your last day of work if relevant. Some people plan to file the month after leaving their job. Make sure your planned end date and your planned filing date line up. Remember that you are considered age 62 on your 62nd birthday. To receive Social Security benefits for a given month, you generally must be 62 for the entire month.

Spousal and family coordination steps:

- Coordinate with your spouse if applicable. If you are married, confirm whether both of you are filing at the same time or at different times. Revisit whether one spouse should delay to increase survivor benefits. Make sure you both understand how each filing date changes the household's long-term income.

- Verify ex-spouse benefit eligibility if divorced. If you were married for at least 10 years and are currently unmarried, you may be eligible for benefits on your ex-spouse's record. Confirm that you meet the requirements before choosing between your own benefit and an ex-spouse benefit.

Medicare coordination steps:

- Confirm Medicare enrollment timing. If you are filing for Social Security at age 65 or later, you will typically be enrolled in Medicare Part A automatically. If you are already receiving Social Security when you turn 65, enrollment is automatic. If you file before 65, you will need to enroll in Medicare separately when the time comes. Review your Initial Enrollment Period (IEP), so you do not trigger late-enrollment penalties.
- Verify whether you need a Special Enrollment Period. If you are still covered by employer health insurance through your own job or your spouse's job, you may qualify for a Special Enrollment Period (SEP) that allows you to delay Medicare Part B without penalty. Confirm the rules at Medicare.gov.

Tax planning confirmation:

- Review your expected income in the year you begin benefits. Up to 85% of your Social Security benefits may be taxable depending on your combined income. Confirm whether your provisional income will exceed the thresholds that trigger taxation.
- Check for Income-Related Monthly Adjustment Amount (IRMAA) exposure. If your Modified Adjusted Gross Income (MAGI) from two years prior exceeds certain thresholds, you will pay higher Medicare Part B and Part D premiums. Plan income accordingly in the years around your filing date.

Mistake Alert: Many applicants focus only on the Social Security claiming decision and miss how the timing affects Medicare enrollment, tax brackets, and IRMAA surcharges. These choices interact. A claiming date that looks "best" for Social Security alone can create avoidable costs elsewhere. Check all four areas before you lock anything in.

Navigating the Online Application

Once you have confirmed your decisions and gathered your documents, you are ready to apply. The SSA offers an online application at SSA.gov that most people can complete in 15 to 30 minutes. Here is what to expect.

Before you begin. You will need your my Social Security account credentials, your Social Security number, your birth certificate information, your bank details for direct deposit, and the names and Social Security numbers of your current or former spouse(s) if you are applying for spousal benefits. Have everything within reach before you start.

Step-by-step portal guide. The online application asks you to confirm personal information (name, date of birth, Social Security number), provide your mailing address and phone number, answer questions about your work history for the current and previous year, indicate whether you want to apply for Medicare at the same time (if you are 65 or older), provide direct deposit information, and select your benefit start date.

The system will ask whether you are currently working and how much you expect to earn in the current year. Answer accurately. That estimate is used to determine whether the earnings test applies.

You will also be asked about your marital history. Provide dates of all marriages and divorces. The SSA uses this information to determine whether you or your spouse may qualify for spousal or survivor benefits.

Common application errors. The most frequent errors include choosing the wrong benefit start date (it is not the same as the day you submit the application), entering incorrect earnings estimates for the current year, leaving out a previous marriage that lasted 10 or more years, and misreading the Medicare enrollment questions.

If you spot an error after submitting, call the SSA and request a correction. In some cases, you can withdraw your application within 12 months of filing if you repay all benefits received. After 12 months, withdrawal is no longer an option.

Completion timeline expectations. After you submit your application online, the SSA typically processes it within a few weeks to a couple of months. You may receive a phone call or letter requesting additional documentation. You can check your status through your my Social Security account. Your first payment often arrives one to two months after your benefit start date, depending on your birthday. People born on the 1st through 10th are generally paid on the second Wednesday of the month. Those born on the 11th through 20th are generally paid on the third Wednesday. Those born on the 21st through 31st are generally paid on the fourth Wednesday.

Working with SSA Representatives

The online application works well for straightforward cases. If your situation includes a public pension, foreign work credits, a complicated spousal or survivor claim, or any of the special situations covered in the previous chapter, it may be worth working directly with an SSA representative.

Office visit preparation. You can schedule an appointment at your local Social Security office by calling 1-800-772-1213. Most SSA field offices now require an appointment for in-person visits; walk-ins are accepted in limited situations, but you will have a much better experience by calling to schedule. When you schedule, ask what documents to bring. Show up with every document on your pre-filing list, even items you think will not apply. It is easier to carry extra paperwork than to reschedule because one document was missing.

Bring a written list of questions. Representatives handle a lot of appointments, and meetings move quickly. A written list helps you cover what you came for.

Phone appointment tips. Phone appointments are another option if you cannot easily visit an office. Prep the same way: keep your documents accessible, have your Social Security number ready, and write your questions out ahead of time. Phone calls tend to be shorter than in-person visits, so lead with your most important questions.

Hold times can be long, sometimes more than an hour during busy periods. Early morning calls (shortly after the lines open at 8:00 a.m. local time) and calls on Wednesdays and Thursdays often have shorter waits.

Documentation organization. Whether you meet in person or by phone, organize your documents in the order you expect them to come up. Keep originals and copies separate. The SSA may need to see original documents (such as birth certificates), but will usually return them. If you have to mail documents, send certified copies rather than originals whenever possible.

Take notes during your appointment. Write down the representative's name, the date, and any instructions or next steps. If you receive conflicting information from different representatives, ask for the policy in writing or request to speak with a supervisor.

Helping Aging Parents Navigate the Process

If you are reading this to help a parent or older family member file for Social Security, expect a few extra moving parts. Adult children often end up coordinating benefits for a parent who is overwhelmed by paperwork, uneasy with online steps, or dealing with cognitive or physical limitations.

Representative payee status. If your parent cannot manage their own finances due to mental or physical incapacity, you can apply to become their representative payee. This gives you legal authority to receive their Social Security payments and use the funds for their care. The SSA requires Form SSA-11 (Request to be Selected as Payee) and may request medical documentation of your parent's incapacity. Being a representative payee comes with responsibilities. You must keep records of how the funds are spent and submit an annual accounting report to the SSA.

Authorized representative roles. If your parent can make their own decisions but needs help with paperwork, they can appoint you as their authorized representative using Form SSA-1696 (Claimant's Appointment of a Representative). This lets you communicate with the SSA on their behalf, attend appointments with them or for them, and access information about their claim. It is different from representative payee status because your parent keeps decision-making authority.

Family coordination strategies. Start by reviewing their my Social Security account together. Check the earnings record for accuracy. If they cannot remember passwords or cannot complete online verification, sit with them and help them through it instead of trying to do it entirely on your own. The SSA may need to confirm that your parent agrees to your involvement.

Gather documents on your parent's behalf: birth certificate, marriage certificates, death certificate for a deceased spouse, military records, and pension information. Many older adults keep important papers in places they no longer remember, or in filing systems that have not been touched in years. Start the search early.

If your parent has limited English proficiency, the SSA provides interpreters at no cost for in-person and phone appointments. Request an interpreter when scheduling.

Mistake Alert: Adult children sometimes file on behalf of a parent without confirming the parent's wishes about timing. A parent who plans to keep working part-time may not want to file yet if the earnings test would reduce benefits. Confirm your parent's broader financial picture and preferences before you start an application.

Chapter Checklist and Verification Tips

Key reminders: Create your my Social Security account well before your planned filing date. Review your earnings record for errors and report discrepancies immediately. Gather required documents 60 to 90 days in advance. Confirm your filing age, benefit estimate, Medicare coordination, and tax implications before submitting. The online application can take 15 to 30 minutes, but only if you are ready when you start.

Most common mistakes: Waiting until filing day to set up a my Social Security account and discovering a name mismatch. Selecting the wrong benefit start date on the application. Forgetting to list a previous marriage that could affect spousal or survivor benefits. Filing for Social Security without coordinating Medicare enrollment timing. Assuming the SSA will catch errors or optimize your benefit for you.

Verification steps before you file:

1. Confirm your my Social Security account is active and your earnings record is accurate
2. Verify you have certified copies of all required documents
3. Confirm your planned benefit start date and understand when your first payment will arrive
4. Review whether the earnings test applies to your situation
5. Coordinate with your spouse on filing timing if applicable
6. Verify Medicare enrollment status and whether you need to enroll separately
7. Check your expected combined income against Social Security taxation thresholds
8. Confirm IRMAA exposure based on your MAGI from two years prior
9. Identify whether you need representative payee or authorized representative status for a family member
10. Write down your questions for the SSA before any appointment

Next steps: Work through this checklist before you submit your application. If something does not line up, fix it first, then file. When you need an answer from the SSA, call with a specific question and keep notes on who you spoke with and what they told you. If your situation includes multiple income sources, a public pension, or complicated spousal planning, consider hiring a fee-only financial planner for a one-time review. Before you act, confirm current-year numbers, deadlines, and thresholds at SSA.gov and Medicare.gov.

11

THE MOST EXPENSIVE SOCIAL SECURITY AND MEDICARE MISTAKES TO AVOID

Every mistake covered in this chapter comes with a price tag. Some cost a few hundred dollars a year. Others can drain tens of thousands over the course of retirement. The gap between a well-timed decision and a poorly timed one often comes down to what you knew, and what you did not, at the exact moment you acted. Here, we put real dollar figures on the most common errors so you can see what is at stake before you file, enroll, or withdraw.

The High Cost of Claiming Early While Working

Claiming Social Security at 62 while you are still earning a solid income sets off two separate rules, and both shrink what you actually take home.

First is the permanent reduction for early filing. If your Full Retirement Age (FRA) is 67, claiming at 62 cuts your monthly benefit by about 30%. On a Primary Insurance Amount (PIA) of $2,000 per month at FRA, you would receive roughly $1,400 instead. That $600 monthly gap lasts for life. Over 20 years of retirement, that is $144,000 in lost income, before Cost-of-Living Adjustments (COLA) are even factored in.

Then comes the earnings test. If you claim before FRA and keep working, the Social Security Administration (SSA) withholds $1 for every $2 you earn above the annual exempt amount. For 2026, that threshold is $24,480 (verify the current-year amount at SSA.gov as it adjusts annually). A worker earning $60,000 a year while claiming at 62 could have roughly $19,000 in benefits withheld over the year. Those withheld benefits are eventually credited back after FRA, but the cash flow hit is real, and the early-filing reduction is still permanent.

And the opportunity cost stacks up fast. If you waited until 70 instead of claiming at 62, your benefit would be about 77% higher than the age-62 amount. On a $1,400 early benefit, delaying to 70 could produce roughly $2,480 per month. That is $1,080 more per month, or $12,960 more per year, for as long as you live.

Mistake Alert: People who claim early while working often say they want to "get what's mine." Here is what that choice typically buys: a permanently reduced benefit, plus temporary withholding that creates confusion and frustration, while the larger benefit you could have earned keeps rising through delayed retirement credits of about 8% per year.

Medicare Enrollment Penalty Costs

Medicare late enrollment penalties are easy to calculate, which is part of what makes them sting. Once the penalty is triggered, you see the cost every month, and it does not quietly fade away.

Part B penalty examples. The Part B late enrollment penalty adds 10% to your standard monthly premium for each full 12-month period you could have enrolled but did not. Suppose the standard Part B premium is $202.90 per month (confirm the current-year amount at Medicare.gov). If you delayed enrollment by two years without qualifying for a Special Enrollment Period (SEP), your penalty is 20%, or about $40.58 per month. That is roughly $487 per year. Over 20 years of Medicare coverage, that one error costs about $9,740.

A three-year delay carries a 30% penalty, adding $60.87 per month, or $730 per year. Over 20 years, that is $14,610. A five-year delay produces a 50% penalty, adding $101.45 per month, or $1,217 per year. Over two decades, that is $24,348.

Part D penalty accumulation. The Medicare Part D late enrollment penalty is 1% of the national base beneficiary premium for each full month without creditable coverage. If the national base premium is approximately $36.78 per month and you went 24 months without coverage, your penalty is 24% of that base, roughly $8.83 per month. That sounds minor at first. But it recalculates as the base premium rises each year, and Medicare Part D late enrollment penalties never expire. Over 15 or 20 years, it can easily total $2,000 or more.

Delaying both Part B and Part D without qualifying coverage can mean combined penalties above $50 per month indefinitely. If both spouses in a household miss their windows, that can turn into $100+ per month with no end date.

Lifetime financial impact. These penalties are permanent add-ons to your premiums. They do not drop off after a few years. They do not shrink as you get older. And when premiums rise, the increases apply to your already-penalized amount, widening the gap over time. Your best protection is enrolling during your Initial Enrollment Period (IEP) or using an eligible enrollment window. Special Enrollment Periods for Medicare require active employer coverage at a company with 20 or more employees.

Spousal Coordination Failures

When married couples make Social Security decisions separately, the household often gives up income that basic coordination could have protected. The losses usually show up in two places: monthly income while both spouses are alive, and the survivor benefit after the first spouse dies.

Household income losses. Consider a couple where the higher earner has a PIA of $2,800 and the lower earner has a PIA of $1,200. If the higher earner claims at 62, their benefit drops to roughly $1,960. If they had waited until 70, it would have grown to about $3,472. The difference is $1,512 per month, or $18,144 per year. Over 15 years of joint retirement, that gap totals more than $272,000 in foregone household income.

Meanwhile, spousal benefits can be equal to up to 50% of the higher earner's PIA at FRA. When the higher earner claims early, the base used to calculate the spousal benefit does not change, but the household strategy often breaks down anyway. The couple may fail to sequence claims in a way that maximizes total lifetime income, especially when one benefit is much larger than the other.

Survivor benefit reduction. The survivor benefit is based on what the deceased spouse was actually receiving (or entitled to receive) at the time of death. If the higher earner claimed at 62 and locked in a reduced benefit of $1,960, the surviving spouse's benefit is tied to that amount. If the higher earner had waited until 70, the survivor could receive roughly $3,472 per month instead. That $1,512 monthly difference can continue for 10, 15, or even 20 years.

If the surviving spouse lives 15 years after their partner's death, the cost of the higher earner claiming early can exceed $270,000 in lost survivor income.

Poor timing consequences. Couples who both claim at 62 without talking through coordination often leave the most money on the table. A common approach is for the lower earner to claim earlier while the higher earner delays, so there is some income coming in while the larger check keeps growing. Ignoring that sequencing is one of the costliest coordination errors couples make. The total household cost, combining reduced lifetime benefits and reduced survivor benefits, can run $200,000 to $400,000, depending on life expectancy and benefit amounts.

IRMAA Triggers from Large Withdrawals

The Income-Related Monthly Adjustment Amount (IRMAA) is a surcharge added to Medicare Part B and Part D premiums when your Modified Adjusted Gross Income (MAGI) crosses certain thresholds. IRMAA uses a two-year lookback period to determine Medicare premium surcharges.

Surcharge amounts by income. IRMAA runs in tiers. At the lowest surcharge tier, which has historically started around $109,000 for single filers and $218,000 for married couples filing jointly (verify current thresholds at Medicare.gov), the extra Part B cost is about $81.20 per month per person. Part D adds roughly $14.50 more. For a married couple where both spouses are on Medicare, that is around $191 per month, or close to $2,300 per year in added premiums.

At higher tiers, the bill climbs quickly. Middle tiers can add $203 to $325.20 per month per person for Part B alone. At the highest tier, the combined Part B and Part D surcharge can exceed $578 per month per person. A couple in that top tier could pay more than $13,900 per year above standard Medicare premiums.

Multi-year penalty cycles. IRMAA is set annually, but the two-year lookback means one income spike can raise premiums for an entire future year. Timing matters more than most people expect. Sell a property in December and close in January, and that income lands on a different tax return, which changes which year your premiums jump. One poorly timed event can turn into 12 months of higher premiums down the road.

It can get worse when the spikes come in back-to-back years. A Roth conversion in year one and a property sale in year two, for example, can trigger IRMAA for two consecutive years. Each year's surcharge is calculated separately, based on that year's lookback return.

Withdrawal timing impact. David's story from Chapter 8 shows this clearly. His $120,000 IRA withdrawal to pay off a mortgage pushed him into the second IRMAA tier. He and his wife paid about $3,600 more in Medicare premiums that year. If he had spread the withdrawal across three years at $40,000 each, he likely would have stayed below the IRMAA threshold, saving the full $3,600 while still paying off the mortgage on his schedule.

Before you take a large distribution, sell an asset, or do a Roth conversion, estimate where your MAGI is likely to land relative to the IRMAA tiers two years from now. A few thousand dollars recognized in the wrong year can turn into a few thousand dollars of Medicare surcharges later (and yes, it is annoying to have to think about a decision today in terms of a bill that shows up two years from now).

Earnings Test Miscalculations

The Social Security earnings test applies to anyone who claims benefits before the FRA while continuing to work. The SSA withholds $1 in benefits for every $2 earned above the annual exempt amount. In the year you reach the FRA, a higher threshold applies, and the withholding rate drops to $1 for every $3 above that threshold.

Benefit withholding amounts. Consider someone claiming $1,800 per month at age 63 while earning $55,000 per year. If the annual exempt amount is $24,480 (confirm the current-year figure at SSA.gov), excess earnings total $30,520. The withholding equals half of that, or $15,260. In practical terms, the SSA would withhold about nine months of benefits during the year. The person expected $21,600 in annual Social Security income and received only about $5,260.

Self-employment surprises. Self-employed individuals face extra complexity. Net earnings from self-employment count toward the earnings test, and the calculation is based on the calendar year. That timing can make income harder to predict. A freelancer or consultant who has one unusually strong year can trigger withholding they did not see coming. Some self-employed retirees also miss that net self-employment income can affect both the earnings test and their combined income for Social Security taxation, creating a double hit.

Income management failures. Some people plan to earn "just under" the exempt amount, then take on extra work, sell a business asset, or receive a year-end bonus that pushes them over. The SSA requires you to report earnings, and discrepancies can create overpayments that must be repaid. Others fail to report expected income accurately when they first claim, so withholding notices show up months later, after the money has already been spent.

Mistake Alert: Benefits withheld under the earnings test are eventually credited back after FRA through a recalculated monthly amount. You do not permanently lose those withheld funds. But the cash flow disruption, the confusion, and the way this interacts with the permanent early-filing reduction still make it one of the most misunderstood parts of early claiming.

Total Financial Impact Analysis

Add up the costs across these categories, and the totals get hard to shrug off.

Cumulative mistake costs. A single retiree who claims early while working, misses their Medicare enrollment window by two years, and takes one large IRA withdrawal that triggers IRMAA can easily rack up $50,000 to $100,000 in combined costs over a 20-year retirement. For a married couple making several uncoordinated decisions, including a weak spousal claiming strategy and missed Medicare deadlines, the total can climb to $200,000 to $400,000 in lost benefits, penalties, surcharges, and tax consequences.

This is not abstract. It is money that would otherwise be available for housing, medical costs, travel, or simply keeping more flexibility later, when it is harder to replace income.

Prevention value proposition. Avoiding these mistakes usually costs far less than making them. A few hours spent reviewing your Social Security statement, running benefit estimates at different claiming ages, confirming your Medicare enrollment timeline, and projecting combined income before a large withdrawal can protect tens of thousands of dollars.

Professional help decision points. If your situation includes multiple income sources, a public pension, tricky spousal coordination, or assets that require large distributions, a one-time consultation with a fee-only financial planner often runs $500 to $3,000. Stack that against the five- and six-figure mistake costs above. When the decisions are hard to unwind, paying for competent advice is often the cheaper option.

EXPENSIVE MISTAKES AND POTENTIAL CONSEQUENCES

Avoiding common Social Security and Medicare mistakes can protect your income, benefits, and peace of mind.

MISTAKE	WHAT CAN HAPPEN	POTENTIAL COST OR IMPACT	HOW TO PREVENT IT
1 Claiming Early Without a Strategy	• Permanently lower monthly benefit • Less income for life	Up to 30% less per month ($100s per month for life)	✓ Understand your break-even age ✓ Compare 62 vs. FRA vs. 70
2 Missing Medicare Enrollment Deadlines	• Late enrollment penalties • Gaps in coverage	10% premium penalty for each 12-month period you delay (Part B)	✓ Know your Initial Enrollment Period ✓ Sign up on time
3 Not Coordinating Spousal Benefits	• Lower household lifetime income • Missed opportunity for higher spousal or survivor benefit	$100s to $1,000s less per month over your lifetime	✓ Compare spousal claiming strategies ✓ Let the higher earner delay if possible
4 Triggering IRMAA Surcharges	• Higher Medicare Part B and Part D premiums • Unexpected annual increases	$1,000s per year in additional premiums (income-based)	✓ Manage income in the 2-year look-back period ✓ Plan withdrawals and conversions
5 Working Past Earnings Test Limits (Before FRA)	• Benefits temporarily withheld • Possible tax-time surprise	$1 withheld for every $2 earned over the limit (before FRA)	✓ Know the annual earnings limits ✓ Report earnings accurately
6 Not Checking Your Earnings Record	• Missing or incorrect earnings • Lower benefits than expected	$100s per month if errors are not corrected	✓ Review your record annually ✓ Dispute errors early
7 Ignoring Survivor Benefit Planning	• Lower surviving spouse benefit • Claiming too early or wrong strategy	$100s per month less for surviving spouse	✓ Understand survivor options ✓ Consider waiting for higher benefit

KEY TAKEAWAY: Small decisions today can have a big financial impact for the rest of your life. Take the time to plan, verify, and coordinate to protect your benefits and your future.

Chapter Checklist and Warning Signs

Red flag indicators that a costly mistake may be approaching:

- You are considering claiming Social Security while earning more than the annual exempt amount
- You have not checked your Medicare enrollment deadline, and you are within six months of turning 65
- You and your spouse have not discussed who should claim first or at what age
- You are planning a withdrawal, conversion, or asset sale exceeding $50,000 in a single year
- You have a public pension and are unsure whether prior WEP or GPO reductions to your Social Security benefit have been correctly removed under the Social Security Fairness Act
- You are relying on COBRA coverage and assuming it protects you from Medicare penalties

Professional consultation triggers: If more than one of the red flags above applies to your situation, or if the total dollar amount at risk exceeds $50,000 over your expected retirement, a fee-only financial advisor or Social Security planning specialist can help you model the outcomes before you act.

Complexity thresholds: If you are coordinating different claiming ages between spouses, managing IRMAA across multiple income sources, or dealing with early claiming while still working, you are in the zone where professional guidance often pays for itself quickly.

12

YOUR PERSONAL RETIREMENT BENEFITS ACTION PLAN

Everything covered so far leads here: building a strategy that fits your situation, your household, your timeline, and your tolerance for complexity. Knowing the rules matters. Knowing the common mistakes matters, too. But rules and warnings only help if they turn into a clear sequence of actions tied to real dates on your calendar. This chapter helps you build that sequence, set up habits that keep your plan current, identify where to get reliable information, and decide when professional guidance is worth paying for.

Creating Your Personalized Claiming Strategy

Your retirement benefits strategy is a chain of connected decisions, not one big choice. It includes when to claim Social Security, how to coordinate with a spouse (if applicable), when to enroll in Medicare, how to manage income to control taxes and Income-Related Monthly Adjustment Amount (IRMAA) surcharges, and which documents and accounts to keep up to date. Treating each piece in isolation is exactly how the expensive mistakes from the previous chapter happen.

Individual situation assessment. Start by writing down the facts that shape your options. What is your Full Retirement Age (FRA)? What does your Social Security statement show as your estimated benefit at 62, FRA, and 70? Are you still working, and if so, how long do you expect to keep going? Do you have a spouse whose benefit is much higher or lower than yours? Are you divorced, widowed, or receiving a public pension? Do you have large traditional IRA or 401(k) balances that will eventually require distributions?

These facts are your foundation. If they are not written down clearly, the rest turns into guesswork.

PERSONAL RETIREMENT BENEFITS ACTION PLAN

Your plan. Your numbers. Your decisions. Take action today for a more secure tomorrow.

1. MY PERSONAL INFORMATION

Name: ______ Date: ______ Birth Date: ______

Spouse/Partner Name: ______ Birth Date: ______

2. MY KEY NUMBERS

My Full Retirement Age (FRA): ______

My Estimated Monthly Benefit at FRA: $ ______

My Estimated Benefit at Age 62: $ ______

My Estimated Benefit at Age 70: $ ______

Spouse/Partner FRA: ______

Spouse/Partner Estimated Benefit at FRA: $ ______

(Use your my Social Security account or the worksheets in this book to fill in your numbers.)

3. MY CLAIMING STRATEGY
(Check Your Plan)

I plan to claim my Social Security benefit at:

- ☐ Age 62 (earliest possible)
- ☐ Full Retirement Age (FRA)
- ☐ Between FRA and Age 70
- ☐ Age 70 (maximum monthly benefit)
- ☐ Still deciding

Why this strategy makes sense for me:

______

4. MY SPOUSAL & SURVIVOR STRATEGY
(Check Your Plan)

Our plan for spousal benefits:

- ☐ File for spousal benefits at my FRA
- ☐ Let higher earner claim first
- ☐ Coordinate claiming for maximum lifetime benefit
- ☐ Still deciding

Our survivor plan:

- ☐ Higher earner will delay for survivor benefit
- ☐ Lower earner will delay (if appropriate)
- ☐ Understand survivor benefit options
- ☐ Still deciding / Need more information

Note: Strategies like "file and suspend" are no longer generally available. "Restricted application" is only available to individuals born before January 2, 1954. Consult SSA.gov for details.

5. MY MEDICARE PLAN
(Check Your Plan)

I plan to enroll in Medicare:

- ☐ At age 65 during my Initial Enrollment Period
- ☐ Before age 65 (due to disability or other reason)
- ☐ Delay Part B (covered by employer plan)
- ☐ Other: ______
- ☐ Still deciding

Medicare coverage I plan to have:

- ☐ Original Medicare (Parts A & B)
- ☐ Medicare Advantage (Part C)
- ☐ Prescription Drug Plan (Part D)
- ☐ Still deciding

6. MY TAX & IRMAA PLAN
(Check Your Plan)

To help manage taxes and IRMAA, I plan to:

- ☐ Review my income sources
- ☐ Manage retirement account withdrawals
- ☐ Use tax-efficient strategies
- ☐ Monitor my 2-year look-back income (IRMAA)
- ☐ Other: ______
- ☐ Still deciding

Notes / My Plan: ______

7. MY NEXT STEPS
Action Items

- ☐ Check my Social Security earnings record
- ☐ Create / Log in to my Social Security account
- ☐ Run my official benefit estimates
- ☐ Review claiming strategy with spouse/partner
- ☐ Review Medicare enrollment timeline
- ☐ Review tax strategy / IRMAA planning
- ☐ Gather documents I will need
- ☐ Talk with a financial or tax professional
- ☐ Other: ______

MY COMMITMENT

I commit to making informed decisions and taking action on my retirement benefits plan.

Signature: ______ Date: ______

IMPORTANT REMINDER

Review your plan at least once a year or when your situation changes. Rules, limits, and your personal circumstances can change. Stay informed and protect the benefits you've earned.

Priority ranking process. Once your facts are on paper, rank your priorities. For some people, maximizing lifetime income is the top goal. For others, it is protecting a surviving spouse's monthly check. If someone has health concerns, the priority might be getting income flowing sooner. For a couple with a large age gap, it may be about bridging the income gap between the first and second retirement dates.

There is no universal right answer. The right answer depends on what matters most to you and which risks you are least willing to live with. Write down your top two priorities. From this point on, each decision should serve those priorities first.

Decision timeline creation. Map your key dates. When do you turn 62? When is your FRA? When do you turn 65 and need to address Medicare? When does your spouse hit those milestones? If you plan to stop working at a specific age, mark that date. If Required Minimum Distributions begin at a certain age for you, mark that too.

Then work backward. If you want benefits to start the month you turn 67, plan to apply early. The Social Security Administration (SSA) recommends applying up to four months before your benefit start date. If you need to enroll in Medicare at 65, your Initial Enrollment Period (IEP) begins three months before your birthday month. Every major decision comes with a preparation window. Put those windows on a calendar now, while you are thinking clearly, instead of scrambling when a deadline is only weeks away.

Essential Websites and Resources

Retirement benefit rules change. Thresholds adjust annually with inflation. Medicare premiums shift. Earnings test limits update. The numbers printed in any guide, including this one, are snapshots. Before you act, verify the current-year figures.

Current-year verification sources. Three official websites cover nearly everything you need:

- SSA.gov provides your earnings record, benefit estimates, the current earnings test limit, Cost-of-Living Adjustment (COLA) announcements, and your application portal.
- Medicare.gov shows current Part B and Part D premiums, IRMAA thresholds, enrollment period dates, and plan comparison tools.
- IRS.gov publishes the income thresholds for Social Security taxation, standard deduction amounts, and tax bracket updates that matter for retirement income planning.

Calculator and tool access. The SSA offers several free calculators. The SSA Retirement Estimator uses actual earnings records to project benefits. The life expectancy calculator can help with break-even analysis. (Note: the WEP and GPO calculators previously offered for non-covered pension situations are no longer needed for benefits payable after December 2023, since both provisions were repealed by the Social Security Fairness Act.) Medicare.gov includes a plan finder tool for Part D and Medicare Advantage options.

Official information channels. When you read something about Social Security or Medicare online, check the source. Official .gov websites are the most reliable places to confirm current rules and figures. Be cautious with news articles, social media posts, or YouTube videos that use outdated numbers or flatten complex rules into a sound bite. If you see a claim about a new rule or benefit change, verify it at SSA.gov or Medicare.gov before you make decisions based on it.

Annual Review Habit Development

Filing for Social Security and enrolling in Medicare are not the end of the process. Income changes. Tax laws shift. Medicare premiums adjust. Your health status and living situation can change, sometimes quickly. A strategy that fit at 66 might need a tweak at 70 or 75. An annual review habit keeps small changes from quietly piling up into a real problem.

Review schedule creation. Pick a consistent time each year for your benefits review. The SSA announces the annual Cost-of-Living Adjustment (COLA) in October or November. The Centers for Medicare & Medicaid Services releases updated premiums around the same time. Other people choose January because new thresholds take effect at the start of the calendar year. The exact month matters less than consistency. Block two to three hours on your calendar and treat it like a financial physical.

Key metrics monitoring. During your annual review, check the following:

- Your total income for the year and how it compares to IRMAA thresholds two years from now.
- Your Medicare plan costs and whether your prescriptions or providers are still covered, and whether the earnings test limit has changed (relevant if you are still working before FRA).
- Your Social Security benefit statement for accuracy.
- Any upcoming Required Minimum Distributions that might push your income into a higher tax or IRMAA bracket.

Change adaptation strategies. When something shifts, decide whether it needs action now or can wait until your next scheduled review. A Medicare formulary change might require action during open enrollment. A jump in income from an unexpected asset sale might call for a life-changing event appeal to reduce IRMAA. A COLA increase might nudge your tax exposure. Small changes get noted for next year. Bigger changes should be addressed promptly, ideally within 30 days, so you stay inside enrollment and appeal windows.

Adapting to Rule Changes

Congress occasionally modifies Social Security and Medicare rules. Premiums and thresholds adjust every year. The SSA's administrative process can shift without much fanfare. Staying current does not require daily monitoring. It does require knowing where to look and how to judge whether a change affects you.

Information source reliability. Rank your sources. Government websites (.gov) are the best for current rules. Established financial planning organizations and fee-only advisor networks often provide solid interpretation when the rules shift. News coverage varies widely in accuracy. Social media posts and forwarded emails are usually the least reliable, and they are also where scams spread fastest. The SSA and Medicare both publish ongoing scam alerts. Before you adjust your strategy based on something you read, ask a simple question: Does this come from a .gov source, or does it clearly cite one?

Update impact assessment. When a rule changes, ask three questions. Does this apply to my situation? Does it affect a decision I have already made, or one I still need to make? Does it require action before a deadline? Most annual adjustments, like a modest COLA increase or a slight rise in the earnings test limit, do not require you to do anything. They just update the numbers you track. Bigger shifts, like changes to IRMAA brackets or Medicare enrollment rules, can affect timing and income management.

Strategy modification process. If a change does require action, go back to your priority ranking. Does the change touch your top two priorities? If it does, check whether your current plan still supports those priorities or needs an adjustment. Run updated numbers using the SSA calculators. If it starts to feel complicated, or if a meaningful amount of money is on the line, that is a reasonable moment to bring in a professional instead of guessing.

The goal is to respond thoughtfully, not react to headlines. Social Security change stories often sound bigger than the real, day-to-day impact on an individual household. Verify first. Then decide.

Professional Advice Guidelines

Some retirement benefit decisions are straightforward enough to handle on your own with the tools and knowledge covered in these chapters. Others involve enough complexity, overlap between systems, or dollars at risk that professional guidance can pay for itself.

When to seek help. Consider professional advice if more than one of the red flags from the previous chapter applies to you: coordinating spousal benefits across different claiming ages, managing IRMAA exposure with multiple income sources, holding a public pension and being unsure whether prior WEP or GPO adjustments have been correctly removed from your benefit, planning large Roth conversions, or handling survivor benefit timing after a spouse's death. If the total dollars at risk exceed $50,000, which is a reasonable estimate in common scenarios, the cost of advice is usually justified relative to the potential savings.

How to choose advisors. Look for fee-only financial planners who specialize in retirement income planning or Social Security claiming decisions. "Fee-only" means they are paid directly by you for advice, rather than earning commissions from selling financial products. That structure reduces conflicts of interest. Ask whether they hold a CFP (Certified Financial Planner) designation, whether they have specific training in Social Security claiming strategies, and how many retirement-focused clients they serve.

You can find fee-only advisors through the National Association of Personal Financial Advisors (NAPFA), the XY Planning Network, or the Garrett Planning Network; all three are well-regarded directories of fee-only advisors. Some advisors offer one-time planning sessions for a flat fee instead of requiring an ongoing relationship.

Cost-benefit analysis. A one-time Social Security and retirement income planning session typically costs $500 to $3,000, depending on complexity and the advisor's experience. Poor timing, missed enrollments, and uncoordinated spousal decisions can cost far more than that in lost benefits and higher premiums, although the exact impact depends on earnings history, lifespan, and the specific mistake. If your situation is complex enough to warrant professional help, paying for it often pencils out. If your situation is simple, such as a single earner with one income source and no spousal coordination, you can usually manage your own plan using the worksheets and checklists provided here.

Family Communication Planning

Retirement benefits affect more than one person, even if only one person files the paperwork. Spouses need to understand each other's claiming plans because those choices directly affect survivor income. Adult children who may eventually help manage a parent's finances need to know where documents are kept and what decisions have already been made. Clear communication prevents confusion later, especially during a health crisis or after a death, when clear thinking is hardest.

Spouse coordination strategies. If you are married, sit down together and review both Social Security statements. Discuss who plans to claim at what age and why. Make sure you both understand how the higher earner's claiming age affects the survivor benefit. Write down your agreed plan, including the specific ages and approximate dates each person intends to file. Revisit it during your annual review.

Adult children involvement. If your adult children are likely to help manage your benefits eventually, share the basics now. Let them know where your Social Security statements, Medicare cards, and tax records are stored. Tell them whether you have a my Social Security account and how to access it if needed. If you have appointed a representative payee or authorized representative, make sure the relevant family members know.

Document sharing systems. Keep one folder, physical or digital, that contains your Social Security statement, Medicare enrollment confirmation, benefit award letters, tax returns from the past two years, and your written claiming strategy. Tell at least one trusted person where it is. Update it annually. If someone has to step in, they should be able to find what they need without hunting for weeks.

At this point, you should be able to do three things: put your key dates on the calendar, confirm the numbers you are using are current, and keep your plan in a place where you and the right people can find it. The rest is execution and a yearly check-in.

CONCLUSION: CLAIM WITH CLARITY, NOT FEAR

Twelve chapters ago, you opened these pages with questions. Some felt urgent. Others were so tangled you may not have known how to say them out loud. Maybe you worried that one wrong move could cost you thousands of dollars, that the system was built to confuse, or that you were already behind and the window for making smart decisions had closed. Those worries are worth naming, because they are exactly what keep a lot of people from acting at all.

You are in a different place now.

What You Now Know That Most Retirees Do Not

Most people file for Social Security without checking their earnings record for mistakes, without understanding how their claiming age permanently changes their monthly amount, and without coordinating the decision with Medicare enrollment or tax planning. You did the work they skipped.

You understand how the 35-year earnings rule feeds into your benefit calculation and why a single zero-earnings year can pull your average down. You know the difference between filing at 62, at your Full Retirement Age (FRA), and at 70, and you can explain why that choice is hard to undo. You understand the earnings test, and you know it is a temporary withholding for people who work before the FRA, not a punishment. You have seen how spousal benefits, survivor benefits, and divorced-spouse benefits each follow their own eligibility rules, and you know which ones apply in your household.

You also know where people get blindsided. You know that missing your Medicare Initial Enrollment Period (IEP) can trigger late-enrollment penalties that follow you for life. You know that Income-Related Monthly Adjustment Amount (IRMAA) surcharges are based on income from two years earlier, which means one unusually high-income year, even from something one-time like selling property, can raise your Medicare premiums later. You know that up to 85% of your Social Security benefits may be taxable if your combined income crosses certain thresholds. And you know that the Social Security Administration (SSA) will not tailor your choice to your situation. They process what you request. The responsibility for informed decisions stays with you.

That puts you ahead of the majority of filers who claim based on a coworker's advice, a scary headline, or simple fear that the rules will change. You have a way to evaluate your own situation and decide based on facts instead of nerves.

Your Three Guiding Principles Going Forward

Knowledge fades if you do not give it a routine. These three principles can keep you steady, whether you file next month or revisit your plan five years from now.

Verify before you act. Every number in these chapters, every threshold, every premium, and every earnings limit is a snapshot of the rules at the time of writing. The Cost-of-Living Adjustment (COLA) changes annually. IRMAA brackets update. Medicare premiums change. Tax thresholds adjust. Before you make any filing decision, check the current-year figures at SSA.gov, Medicare.gov, and IRS.gov. Verify your earnings record in your my Social Security account. Confirm your benefit estimate still matches your plan. Those few minutes of verification can save you months of cleanup paperwork.

Coordinate decisions across Social Security, Medicare, and taxes. These three systems overlap in ways that catch people off guard. A claiming date that gives you the biggest Social Security check can also push your combined income into a range that triggers benefit taxation or IRMAA surcharges. A Medicare enrollment delay that seems reasonable can still create a permanent penalty if you do not qualify for a Special Enrollment Period (SEP). Your personal action plan, built in the previous chapter, treats these as connected choices. Keep treating them that way every time you adjust anything.

Revisit your plan annually as rules and circumstances change. You set up an annual review schedule for a reason. Life changes. Health changes. Congress changes things. A strategy that fits perfectly at 64 might need a small correction at 68 or a bigger one at age 73 (or 75 if you were born in 1960 or later) when Required Minimum Distributions (RMDs) begin under current law. Verify the current RMD age at IRS.gov. Your annual check-in, whether you do it in November when new numbers come out or in January when new thresholds take effect, keeps your plan tied to reality instead of running on autopilot.

They are simple enough to remember without a worksheet. Verify. Coordinate. Revisit. Do that consistently, and you catch most problems while they are still cheap and fixable.

Permission to Move Forward

If you have read this far and still feel the urge to wait, to gather just a little more information before you move, you are not the only one. These systems are complicated, and inaction can feel safer than action. But waiting has a price: missed enrollment windows, earnings records that never get corrected, delayed credits left on the table, or a surviving spouse stuck with a lower benefit because the higher earner kept putting the decision off.

You do not need a flawless strategy. You need a reasonable one, built on accurate numbers, aligned with your priorities, and checked often enough to catch errors while they are still repairable. Perfection is not the standard. Preparation is.

Look at what you have already done in these chapters. You reviewed your earnings history. You know your FRA and how filing age affects your monthly payment. You figured out whether spousal, survivor, or ex-spouse benefits matter in your household. You built a document checklist, a list of questions for the SSA, and a plan for Medicare enrollment. You mapped out how income sources interact with taxes and IRMAA. That is more prep than most people do before they click "submit."

Progress beats paralysis. If your plan is 90% ready and you are stuck on the last 10%, ask yourself what waiting another year costs in dollars and in mental bandwidth. Sometimes waiting truly serves you because delayed credits are worth it. Other times, waiting serves nothing except fear. It helps to say the quiet part out loud and decide which one you are dealing with.

Confidence here does not come from predicting the future. Nobody knows how long they will live, what Congress will do next, or whether health costs will rise faster than expected. Confidence comes from knowing how the rules work today, knowing your numbers today, and having a plan you are willing to adjust. That is the whole job.

Final Words and Encouragement

You earned these benefits. Every year on your earnings record represents real work, real time, and real payroll taxes paid into a system meant to replace income when you stop working. Claiming Social Security is not a favor. It is money you funded over decades. Treat the process that way: clearly, carefully, and without apology.

Filing is not a test you can fail if you plan. The expensive mistakes covered earlier almost always come from acting without the right information or missing deadlines. You already have the information. You know the deadlines. You have a checklist, a timeline, a written strategy, and your documents ready to go. That is what separates a stressful filing from a straightforward one.

Now pick the next step and put a date on it. If your filing window is months away, block the prep tasks on your calendar. If you are filing soon, run your before-you-file checklist one more time and confirm the numbers you are using are current. If you are helping a parent or spouse, sit down together and go line by line through statements and dates. If your situation is complicated enough to justify a professional review, book it and bring your paperwork.

The system is complicated. Your next action does not have to be. Verify your current figures, confirm your dates, and file when your plan says to file.

BONUS SECTION: CURRENT-YEAR NUMBERS AND VERIFICATION GUIDE

Every figure mentioned throughout these chapters, from earnings test limits to IRMAA thresholds to Medicare premiums, changes on a schedule set by federal agencies. Congress adjusts some numbers through legislation; others move automatically with inflation. So any specific dollar amount printed today can be outdated by next January. Instead of handing you numbers that may mislead you a year from now, this section shows you where to look, what to confirm, and how to build a simple once-a-year habit that keeps your planning current.

Where to Find Updated Numbers Each Year

Three official sources publish the figures that matter most for Social Security, Medicare, and retirement tax planning. Bookmark all three.

SSA.gov is where the Social Security Administration (SSA) announces the annual Cost-of-Living Adjustment (COLA) each October. That same announcement usually includes updated earnings test limits, the maximum taxable earnings cap, and the dollar amount needed to earn one work credit. To find it, search "COLA" on SSA.gov or pull up the annual fact sheet the agency publishes each fall.

Medicare.gov and CMS typically publish updated Part B and Part D standard premiums in October or November for the following calendar year. This is also where you will find the current Income-Related Monthly Adjustment Amount (IRMAA) income tiers and the surcharge amounts tied to each tier. The Centers for Medicare & Medicaid Services (CMS) issues a formal announcement, and Medicare.gov updates its pages to match.

IRS.gov is where you verify federal tax bracket boundaries, the combined income thresholds that determine whether Social Security benefits are taxable, standard deduction amounts, and Required Minimum Distribution (RMD) tables. Look for IRS Publication 915 (Social Security and equivalent benefits), Publication 590-B (Distributions from Individual Retirement Arrangements (IRAs), and the annual revenue procedures that update inflation-adjusted figures. Most of these are finalized by November for the following tax year.

Official Websites & Current-Year Numbers to Verify

Use this page to track the official sources and annual numbers you should verify before filing for benefits, enrolling in Medicare, or making major retirement income decisions.

1. Official Websites to Use

Website	Best Use	What to Check
SSA.gov	Social Security benefits, earnings record, claiming ages, spousal and survivor rules, COLA updates	my Social Security account, benefit estimates, earnings test limits, maximum taxable earnings, current rules
Medicare.gov	Medicare enrollment, Parts A, B, C, and D, premiums, penalties, plan comparisons	Initial Enrollment Period rules, Part B premium, Part D information, Medicare coverage options
IRS.gov	Taxes on Social Security benefits, retirement withdrawals, withholding, IRMAA-related tax planning context	taxation rules, provisional income guidance, RMD information, current tax forms and instructions

2. Current-Year Numbers to Verify

- Annual earnings limit before Full Retirement Age (FRA): ____________
- Higher earnings limit in the year you reach FRA: ____________
- Maximum taxable earnings for Social Security taxes: ____________
- Social Security COLA for the current year: ____________
- Medicare Part B standard premium: ____________
- Medicare Part B deductible: ____________
- IRMAA income thresholds: ____________
- Social Security taxation thresholds: ____________
- Required Minimum Distribution (RMD) age/rules: ____________
- My key filing or enrollment deadlines this year: ____________

3. My Annual Verification Checklist

- [ ] Log in to my Social Security account
- [ ] Review my earnings record for errors
- [ ] Check my updated benefit estimates
- [ ] Verify Medicare premiums and enrollment rules
- [ ] Review current IRS tax guidance
- [ ] Recheck IRMAA thresholds before large withdrawals
- [ ] Update this page once a year
- [ ] Verify numbers again before filing

4. My Notes

____

____

____

____

____

____

____

____

Important Reminder

Social Security, Medicare, and tax numbers can change each year. Always verify current figures and rules through official government websites before making a filing or retirement income decision.

Key Numbers to Verify Before Filing

Before you file for Social Security, update your retirement withdrawal plan for a new year, or make a Medicare enrollment decision, verify these figures against current official sources:

Earnings test limits. If you plan to collect Social Security before your Full Retirement Age (FRA) while still working, you need the current annual earnings limit. This number determines how much you can earn before the SSA temporarily withholds part of your benefit. It rises most years. The limit is different in the year you reach FRA than it is in earlier years, and both numbers appear in the SSA's annual COLA announcement.

IRMAA income thresholds. These tiers determine whether you will pay a surcharge on your Medicare Part B and Part D premiums. Because IRMAA uses a two-year lookback, you need to know both the current year's thresholds for the premiums you pay now and the thresholds that will apply based on this year's income. Medicare.gov publishes the tiers, and the SSA also includes them in its annual notices.

Full Retirement Age by birth year. Your FRA depends on when you were born and does not change from year to year for you personally. Still, if you are helping a parent or spouse whose birth year differs from yours, confirm their exact FRA. SSA.gov has a calculator that provides the specific month and year.

Maximum taxable earnings cap. This is the ceiling on earnings subject to Social Security payroll taxes in a given year. If you are still working and earn above the cap, only earnings up to that amount count toward the benefit formula. It typically rises each year.

Medicare Part B and Part D standard premiums. Even if you are not subject to IRMAA, you still need the base premium amounts for budgeting. Part B premiums are usually deducted directly from your Social Security check, so an increase can shrink your net deposit.

How to Set Up Annual Verification Reminders

Most of the key announcements arrive in a fairly predictable window. Social Security's COLA announcement typically comes in the second week of October. Medicare premium updates often arrive around the same time, sometimes a bit earlier. IRS inflation adjustments for the following tax year are usually finalized by early November.

Set two calendar reminders. Put the first in the second week of October with a note to check SSA.gov for the COLA announcement and Medicare.gov for premium updates. Set the second for mid-November to check IRS.gov for updated tax brackets, standard deductions, and any changes affecting RMDs. (If you like specific dates, October 10 and November 15 are usually close enough to catch the updates without waiting until the holidays.)

When those reminders pop up, give yourself fifteen minutes to refresh your personal numbers. Recalculate your projected combined income for the coming year using the new thresholds. See whether your Modified Adjusted Gross Income (MAGI) is near an IRMAA tier boundary. If it is, adjust your withdrawal plan or Roth conversion approach when the updated figures make a meaningful difference.

If you work with a financial advisor or tax professional, send a brief note after you review the updates. A simple question like, "Do any of these new numbers change what we planned?" can save time and prevent unpleasant surprises.

Why This Section Does Not Print Specific Dollar Amounts

You may have noticed that this section, and much of this guide, avoids printing exact dollar figures for thresholds that change annually. That choice is intentional.

Social Security earnings test limits, IRMAA tiers, Medicare premiums, tax brackets, and the maximum taxable earnings cap all adjust on their own schedules. A number printed today may be wrong by the time you revisit this next year. If you rely on a figure from a page without checking the current amount, you can make an expensive decision based on outdated information.

Verifying current numbers protects you better than memorizing last year's thresholds. The figures move; your process should not. Know where to look and when to look, then update your worksheet before you act.

Treat any dollar figure you see in a retirement resource, including this one, as a starting point. Confirm it on the official site before you file, enroll, convert, or withdraw.

GLOSSARY: SOCIAL SECURITY, MEDICARE, AND TAX TERMS IN PLAIN ENGLISH

This glossary gathers the key terms you have come across in these chapters. Each definition uses plain language, so you can confirm a term quickly without rereading a full section. Keep it handy whenever you run into an acronym or phrase you want to double-check.

Essential Social Security Acronyms

AIME (Average Indexed Monthly Earnings): The inflation-adjusted average of your highest 35 years of earnings, calculated as a monthly figure. The Social Security Administration uses AIME as the starting point for determining your benefit amount. Years with zero earnings bring this average down.

COLA (Cost-of-Living Adjustment): The annual percentage increase applied to Social Security benefits to help them keep pace with inflation. COLA is announced each fall and takes effect the following January. The size of the adjustment varies from year to year and is based on a consumer price index.

DRC (Delayed Retirement Credits): The percentage increase added to your benefit for each month you delay claiming Social Security past your Full Retirement Age, up to age 70. Credits build at roughly two-thirds of one % per month, which works out to about 8% per year of delay.

FRA (Full Retirement Age): The age at which you qualify for 100% of your Primary Insurance Amount. FRA depends on your birth year and falls between 66 and 67 for most people nearing retirement. Filing before FRA permanently reduces your monthly benefit; filing after FRA earns delayed retirement credits.

PIA (Primary Insurance Amount): The monthly benefit you would receive if you claim exactly at your Full Retirement Age. PIA is calculated from your AIME using a formula with bend points. It replaces a higher percentage of lower earnings and a smaller percentage of higher earnings.

SSA (Social Security Administration): The federal agency that runs Social Security programs, processes claims, maintains earnings records, and issues benefit payments.

SSDI (Social Security Disability Insurance): A benefit program for workers who become disabled before reaching retirement age. Eligibility requires enough work credits and a qualifying medical condition. SSDI benefits convert automatically to retirement benefits at Full Retirement Age.

Bend Points: Dollar thresholds in the PIA formula that determine what percentage of your AIME Social Security replaces. Bend points are adjusted each year for inflation. The formula replaces 90% of earnings below the first bend point, 32% between the first and second bend points, and 15% above the second.

Earnings Test: The rule that temporarily reduces Social Security benefits for people who claim before the FRA and continue to earn above a set limit. Withheld benefits are recalculated and credited back after you reach the FRA, so the reduction works more like a deferral than a permanent loss.

Work Credits: Units earned through employment and self-employment that determine eligibility for Social Security benefits. You need 40 credits (roughly 10 years of work) to qualify for retirement benefits. You can earn up to four credits per year.

Windfall Elimination Provision (WEP): A formula adjustment that, prior to its repeal by the Social Security Fairness Act, reduced Social Security retirement benefits for people who also received a pension from work where they did not pay Social Security taxes (such as certain government or foreign employment). WEP was repealed for monthly benefits payable after December 2023.

Government Pension Offset (GPO): A rule that, prior to its repeal by the Social Security Fairness Act, reduced spousal or survivor Social Security benefits for people who received a pension from government work not covered by Social Security. GPO was repealed for monthly benefits payable after December 2023.

Survivor FRA (Full Retirement Age for Survivor Benefits): The age at which a surviving spouse can claim 100% of the survivor benefit without an early-claiming reduction. For most people born in 1962 or later, the survivor FRA is 67; for earlier birth years, it ranges from 66 to 67. Note that survivor FRA can be slightly different from retirement FRA depending on birth year.

Key SSA Forms: Form SSA-44 is used to request a reduction in IRMAA after a life-changing event. Form SSA-1696 (Claimant's Appointment of a Representative) lets you authorize a family member or advisor to act on your behalf. Form SSA-11 is the application to become a representative payee for someone unable to manage their own benefits. Form W-4V is used to set up voluntary federal income tax withholding from Social Security payments.

Medicare Terms and Definitions

Part A (Hospital Insurance): Covers inpatient hospital stays, skilled nursing facility care, hospice, and some home health services. Most people pay no monthly premium for Part A if they or a spouse paid Medicare taxes for at least 40 quarters.

Part B (Medical Insurance): Covers doctor visits, outpatient care, preventive services, and durable medical equipment. Part B requires a monthly premium that is typically deducted from your Social Security check.

Part C (Medicare Advantage): Private insurance plans approved by Medicare that combine Part A and Part B coverage and often include prescription drugs, dental, vision, and hearing benefits. Enrollment requires having both Part A and Part B.

Part D (Prescription Drug Coverage): Standalone plans offered by private insurers that cover outpatient prescription medications. Each plan has its own formulary, premiums, and cost-sharing structure.

IEP (Initial Enrollment Period): The seven-month window centered on your 65th birthday month during which you can enroll in Medicare Parts A and B. Missing this window without qualifying coverage can trigger permanent late-enrollment penalties.

SEP (Special Enrollment Period): A window that lets you enroll in Medicare outside the standard deadlines without a penalty. It is most commonly available to people who had group health coverage through an employer where they or a spouse was actively working.

IRMAA (Income-Related Monthly Adjustment Amount): A surcharge added to Medicare Part B and Part D premiums for beneficiaries whose Modified Adjusted Gross Income exceeds certain thresholds. IRMAA is based on income reported on your tax return from two years earlier.

Medigap (Medicare Supplement Insurance): Private insurance policies that help pay out-of-pocket costs left by Original Medicare, including deductibles, copayments, and coinsurance. Medigap plans are standardized by letter (Plan G, Plan N, etc.) and work only with Original Medicare, not Medicare Advantage.

Creditable Coverage: Prescription drug coverage from an employer, union, or other source that is expected to pay at least as much as Medicare's standard Part D plan. Having creditable coverage protects you from Part D late-enrollment penalties if you delay enrollment.

Medigap Open Enrollment Period: A six-month window that starts when you are both 65 or older and enrolled in Part B. During this period, insurers must sell you a Medigap policy at standard rates without medical underwriting.

Tax-Related Terms for Retirees

AGI (Adjusted Gross Income): Your total income from taxable sources (wages, pensions, traditional IRA withdrawals, rental income, capital gains, and other sources) minus specific deductions such as IRA contributions or student loan interest. AGI appears on your federal tax return and feeds into many retirement-related calculations.

MAGI (Modified Adjusted Gross Income): For Medicare IRMAA purposes, MAGI equals your AGI plus any tax-exempt interest income (such as municipal bond interest). This figure determines whether you owe surcharges on Medicare premiums.

Combined Income (Provisional Income): The formula used to determine whether your Social Security benefits are subject to federal income tax. Combined income equals your AGI, plus nontaxable interest, plus one-half of your Social Security benefits. Crossing $25,000 (single) or $32,000 (married filing jointly) can make up to 50% of benefits taxable. Crossing $34,000 (single) or $44,000 (married filing jointly) can make up to 85% taxable.

RMD (Required Minimum Distribution): The minimum amount you must withdraw each year from traditional IRAs and most employer retirement plans once you reach the applicable RMD age (73 if born between 1951 and 1959; 75 if born in 1960 or later, under current law). Failing to take RMDs on time triggers a significant tax penalty.

Roth Conversion: Moving money from a traditional IRA or 401(k) into a Roth IRA. You pay income tax on the converted amount in the year of the conversion, but qualified Roth withdrawals are generally tax-free afterward and do not count toward combined income or MAGI.

SECA (Self-Employment Contributions Act): The federal tax that self-employed workers pay to fund Social Security and Medicare. The combined SECA rate is 15.3% (12.4% Social Security plus 2.9% Medicare) on net self-employment income, up to the Social Security taxable maximum. Half of SECA is deductible from your AGI.

Quick Reference Key Concepts

Benefit Calculation Basics: Social Security uses your highest 35 years of indexed earnings to calculate your AIME, applies the bend-point formula to determine your PIA, and then adjusts the PIA based on your claiming age.

Enrollment Periods: Medicare's IEP is seven months around your 65th birthday. Medigap open enrollment is six months, starting when you have Part B at age 65 or older. SEPs apply when qualifying employer coverage ends.

Common Penalty Types: The Part B late-enrollment penalty adds 10% to your premium for each full 12-month period of eligible delay. The Part D late-enrollment penalty adds approximately 1% of the national base beneficiary premium for each full month without creditable coverage. Both penalties are generally permanent.

SOURCES

YOUR ROADMAP TO CONFIDENT RETIREMENT DECISIONS

(2024). ssa.gov. https://www.ssa.gov/benefits/retirement/planner/gpo.html

(n.d.). medicare.gov. https://www.medicare.gov/basics/costs/medicare-costs-at-a-glance

(n.d.). ssa.gov. https://www.ssa.gov/oact/quickcalc

(2025-12-13). 247wallst.com. https://247wallst.com/investing/2025/12/13/how-claiming-social-security-early-heres-how-that-might-impact-your-retirement-beyond-the-smaller-monthly-checks

(n.d.). ssa.gov. https://www.ssa.gov/

(n.d.). ssa.gov. https://www.ssa.gov/prepare/review-record-earnings

(2024). ssa.gov. https://www.ssa.gov/benefits/calculators

(n.d.). medicare.gov. https://www.medicare.gov/basics/get-started-with-medicare/sign-up/avoid-penalties

(2026). ssa.gov. https://www.ssa.gov/pubs/EN-05-10069.pdf

(n.d.). ssa.gov. https://www.ssa.gov/myaccount/statement.html

CHAPTER 1: HOW SOCIAL SECURITY REALLY CALCULATES YOUR BENEFITS

(2023). ssa.gov. https://www.ssa.gov/pubs/EN-05-10045.pdf

(2024). ssa.gov. https://www.ssa.gov/pubs/EN-05-10072.pdf

(2025). ssa.gov. https://www.ssa.gov/policy/docs/chartbooks/fast_facts/2025/fast_facts25.html

(2025). ssa.gov. https://www.ssa.gov/news/en/cola/index.html

(n.d.). Social Security COLAs For Ages 60-62. https://www.helpwithmysocialsecurity.com/post/social-security-colas-for-ages-60-62

(n.d.). Ask Larry: Will The COLAs That Occur Before I Reach Age 62 .... https://www.maximizemysocialsecurity.com/ask-larry/will-colas-occur-i-reach-age-62-increase-my-future-benefits

(n.d.). Benefit Calculation Examples for Workers Retiring in 2026. https://www.ssa.gov/oact/progdata/retirebenefit1.html

(n.d.). How Retirement Benefits Are Calculated By Social Security - AARP. https://www.aarp.org/social-security/faq/how-are-benefits-calculated-by-ssa

(n.d.). How Cost-of-Living Adjustments Affect Social Security Benefits. https://cannonfinancialstrategists.com/wp-content/uploads/How-COLAs-Affect-SS-Benefits.pdf

CHAPTER 2: BEFORE YOU CLAIM: CHOOSING THE RIGHT FILING AGE FOR YOUR SITUATION

(2024). ssa.gov. https://www.ssa.gov/oact/STATS/table4c6.html

(n.d.). ssa.gov. https://www.ssa.gov/benefits/retirement/planner/delayret.html

(n.d.). fidelity.com. https://www.fidelity.com/viewpoints/retirement/social-security-myths

(n.d.). ssa.gov. https://www.ssa.gov/survivor

(n.d.). ssa.gov. https://www.ssa.gov/oact/cola/examplemax.html

(2026). ssa.gov. https://www.ssa.gov/oact/cola/Benefits.html

(n.d.). Earn, Baby, Earn: The Key to Maximizing Your Social Security. https://www.hartfordfunds.com/practice-management/client-conversations/financial-planning/earn-baby-earn-the-key-to-maximizing-your-social-security.html

(n.d.). Calculating Delayed Retirement Credits - Support Center - LifeYield. https://help.lifeyield.com/calculating-delayed-retirement-credits

(n.d.). Should I Delay My Railroad Retirement to Get an 8 % Increase?. https://highballadvisors.com/blog/should-i-delay-my-railroad-retirement-to-get-an-8-%-increase

CHAPTER 3: WORKING WHILE CLAIMING: HOW EARNINGS CAN AFFECT YOUR CHECKS

(2024). ssa.gov. https://www.ssa.gov/oact/cola/rtea.html

(2023). ssa.gov. https://www.ssa.gov/policy/docs/program-explainers/retirement-earnings-test.html

(2026). ssa.gov. https://www.ssa.gov/faqs/en/questions/KA-01921.html

(2025). nerdwallet.com. https://www.nerdwallet.com/retirement/learn/how-much-can-you-earn-while-on-social-security

(2026). thrivent.com. https://www.thrivent.com/insights/social-security/how-much-can-you-earn-while-on-social-security

(2023-11-14). secure.ssa.gov. https://secure.ssa.gov/apps10/poms.nsf/lnx/0302505065

(1979). ssa.gov. https://www.ssa.gov/OP_Home/rulings/oasi/35/SSR-79-04-oasi-35.html

(2024). aarp.org. https://www.aarp.org/social-security/faq/how-often-does-ssa-recalculate-benefits

CHAPTER 4: SPOUSAL BENEFITS: HOW COUPLES CAN COORDINATE FOR MORE LIFETIME SECURITY

(2023). ssa.gov. https://www.ssa.gov/pubs/EN-05-10084.pdf

(2023). ssa.gov. https://www.ssa.gov/survivor/amount

(2024). ssa.gov. https://www.ssa.gov/benefits/retirement/planner/claiming.html

(n.d.). ssa.gov. https://www.ssa.gov/oact/quickcalc/spouse.html

(2024). ssa.gov. https://www.ssa.gov/benefits/survivors/ifyou.html

(2024). ssa.gov. https://www.ssa.gov/agency/contact

(n.d.). Social Security spousal benefits: Here's how much spouses can get. https://www.bankrate.com/retirement/social-security-spousal-benefits

(n.d.). The 50% Social Security Spousal Benefit Explained: You Can't Have .... https://www.youtube.com/watch?v=k36PWbglvi8&vl=en

(n.d.). Multiple Marriages and Social Security Survivor Benefits - AARP. https://www.aarp.org/social-security/faq/remarried-former-spouse-dies-eligible-benefits

CHAPTER 5: SURVIVOR BENEFITS: PROTECTING THE SPOUSE WHO MAY LIVE LONGER

(2024). ssa.gov. https://www.ssa.gov/benefits/survivors

(n.d.). ssa.gov. https://www.ssa.gov/benefits/survivors/ifyou.html

(n.d.). ssa.gov. https://www.ssa.gov/benefits/survivors/onyourown.html

(2024). ssa.gov. https://www.ssa.gov/pubs/EN-05-10084.pdf

(n.d.). Survivor Benefits Planner - AARP. https://www.aarp.org/social-security/survivor-benefits

CHAPTER 6: DIVORCE AND SOCIAL SECURITY: BENEFITS YOU MAY NOT KNOW YOU CAN CLAIM

(2024). ssa.gov. https://www.ssa.gov/faqs/en/questions/KA-02035.html

(n.d.). aarp.org. https://www.aarp.org/social-security/divorced-spouse-benefits

(n.d.). ssa.gov. https://www.ssa.gov/family/eligibility

(n.d.). fidelity.com. https://www.fidelity.com/viewpoints/retirement/social-security-for-divorced-spouses

(2024-08-22). ssa.gov. https://www.ssa.gov/blog/en/posts/2024-08-22.html

(2023). investor.vanguard.com. https://investor.vanguard.com/investor-resources-education/social-security/benefits-for-divorced-spouse

(n.d.). ssa.gov. https://www.ssa.gov/forms/ssa-2.html

(2023). mfs.com. https://www.mfs.com/content/dam/mfs-enterprise/mfscom/sales-tools/sales-ideas/mfsp_ssdiv_fly.pdf

(n.d.). peoples-law.org. https://www.peoples-law.org/node/49072/printable/print

CHAPTER 7: MEDICARE AND SOCIAL SECURITY: ENROLLMENT DEADLINES, COVERAGE CHOICES, AND COSTLY PENALTIES

(2024). medicare.gov. https://www.medicare.gov/basics/get-started-with-medicare/get-more-coverage/joining-a-plan

(2026). medicare.gov. https://www.medicare.gov/basics/costs/medicare-costs/avoid-penalties

(Current). anthem.com. https://www.anthem.com/medicare/turning-65

(Current). humana.com. https://www.humana.com/medicare/medicare-resources/medicare-eligibility-age-and-qualifications

(2026). medicare.gov. https://www.medicare.gov/supplements/other-insurance/how-to-compare-medigap-policies

(2024). medicare.gov. https://www.medicare.gov/health-drug-plans/part-b/costs/penalties

(Current). medicare.gov. https://www.medicare.gov/basics/get-started-with-medicare

(2026). medicare.gov. https://www.medicare.gov/basics/get-started-with-medicare/medicare-basics/working-past-65

(2026). medicare.gov. https://www.medicare.gov/health-drug-plans/medigap/medigap-open-enrollment

(2024). medicare.gov. https://www.medicare.gov/basics/get-started-with-medicare/medicare-basics/working-past-65/cobra-coverage

CHAPTER 8: TAXES, IRMAA, AND THE RETIREMENT INCOME TRAPS THAT CAN SHRINK YOUR BENEFITS

(n.d.). ssa.gov. https://www.ssa.gov/faqs/en/questions/KA-02471.html

(2026). medicare.gov. https://www.medicare.gov/publications/11579-medicare-costs.pdf

(Ongoing SSA policy). secure.ssa.gov. https://secure.ssa.gov/poms.nsf/lnx/0601101010

(2024). schwab.com. https://www.schwab.com/learn/story/not-always-tax-free-7-municipal-bond-tax-traps

(n.d.). irs.gov. https://www.irs.gov/retirement-plans/plan-participant-employee/retirement-topics-required-minimum-distributions-rmds

(2026). kiplinger.com. https://www.kiplinger.com/retirement/medicare/medicare-premiums-2026-irmaa-brackets-and-surcharges-for-parts-b-and-d

(n.d.). fidelity.com. https://www.fidelity.com/learning-center/personal-finance/is-social-security-taxed

(n.d.). secure.ssa.gov. https://secure.ssa.gov/poms.nsf/lnx/0601101020

(2026 (current)). medicareresources.org. https://www.medicareresources.org/medicare-eligibility-and-enrollment/what-is-the-income-related-monthly-adjusted-amount-irmaa

(n.d.). irs.gov. https://www.irs.gov/taxtopics/tc403

CHAPTER 9: SPECIAL SITUATIONS: PUBLIC PENSIONS, SELF-EMPLOYMENT, MILITARY SERVICE, DISABILITY, AND FOREIGN WORK

(2026). ssa.gov. https://www.ssa.gov/OP_Home/handbook/handbook.06/handbook-0615.html

(n.d.). irs.gov. https://www.irs.gov/businesses/small-businesses-self-employed/self-employment-tax-social-security-and-medicare-taxes

(2025). ssa.gov. https://www.ssa.gov/international/agreements_overview.html

(2025). ssa.gov. https://www.ssa.gov/benefits/retirement/planner/military.html

(2004). ssa.gov. https://www.ssa.gov/OP_Home/handbook/handbook.09/handbook-0940.html

(n.d.). irs.gov. https://www.irs.gov/taxtopics/tc751

(2026). medicare.gov. https://www.medicare.gov/basics/get-started-with-medicare/medicare-basics/parts-of-medicare

(n.d.). ssa.gov. https://www.ssa.gov/pubs/EN-05-10022.pdf

(2025). ssa.gov. https://www.ssa.gov/benefits/retirement/social-security-fairness-act.html

CHAPTER 10: BEFORE YOU FILE: DOCUMENTS, DEADLINES, ACCOUNTS, AND FINAL CHECKS

(2023). ssa.gov. https://www.ssa.gov/forms/ssa-1696.pdf

(n.d.). ssa.gov. https://www.ssa.gov/benefits/retirement/planner/agereduction.html

(n.d.). ssa.gov. https://www.ssa.gov/oact/progdata/cyclicalpay.html

(2025). ssa.gov. https://www.ssa.gov/myaccount

(2024). ssa.gov. https://www.ssa.gov/payee/faqrep.htm

(n.d.). ssa.gov. https://www.ssa.gov/ssi/text-entitle-ussi.htm

(2026). ssa.gov. https://www.ssa.gov/pubs/EN-05-10031-2026.pdf

(2025-06-07). ssa.gov. https://www.ssa.gov/myaccount/create.html

CHAPTER 11: THE MOST EXPENSIVE SOCIAL SECURITY AND MEDICARE MISTAKES TO AVOID

(2026). schwab.com. https://www.schwab.com/learn/story/guide-on-taking-social-security

(n.d.). maximizemysocialsecurity.com. https://www.maximizemysocialsecurity.com/ask-larry/how-does-social-security-adjust-benefits-withheld-due-earnings-test

(2025). northwesternmutual.com. https://www.northwesternmutual.com/life-and-money/taking-social-security-at-62-vs-67-vs-70

(2025). ssa.gov. https://www.ssa.gov/benefits/retirement/planner/1960.html

(n.d.). Medicare Part D Late Enrollment Penalty: What You Need to Know. https://www.ncoa.org/article/medicare-part-d-late-enrollment-penalty

(n.d.). Collecting Social Security Benefits at 62 vs. 67 vs. 70 - AARP. https://www.aarp.org/social-security/faq/62-vs-67-vs-70

CHAPTER 12: YOUR PERSONAL RETIREMENT BENEFITS ACTION PLAN

(n.d.). irs.gov. https://www.irs.gov/taxtopics/tc423

(2025). napfa.org. https://www.napfa.org/articles/fee-only-planner-costs

(n.d.). napfa.org. https://www.napfa.org/public/when-to-hire-a-planner

(2026). napfa.org. https://www.napfa.org/find-an-advisor

(2026). napfa.org. https://www.napfa.org/what-is-fee-only

(2025). ssa.gov. https://www.ssa.gov/benefits/retirement/planner/wep.html

(2023-10-30). ssa.gov. https://www.ssa.gov/news/press/releases/2023/20231030.html

CONCLUSION: CLAIM WITH CLARITY, NOT FEAR

(2024). ssa.gov. https://www.ssa.gov/benefits/retirement/planner/whileworking.html

(2024). irs.gov. https://www.irs.gov/newsroom/irs-reminds-taxpayers-their-social-security-benefits-may-be-taxable

(2024). ssa.gov. https://www.ssa.gov/benefits/medicare/medicare-premiums.html

(2024). irs.gov. https://www.irs.gov/retirement-plans/plan-participant-employee/required-minimum-distribution-worksheets

(2024). ssa.gov. https://www.ssa.gov/cola

GLOSSARY: SOCIAL SECURITY, MEDICARE, AND TAX TERMS IN PLAIN ENGLISH

(2022). cms.gov. https://www.cms.gov/outreach-and-education/outreach/partnerships/downloads/11222-p.pdf

(2026). cms.gov. https://www.cms.gov/medicare/enrollment-renewal/original-part-a-b

(n.d.). hrblock.com. https://www.hrblock.com/tax-center/income/retirement-income/how-much-social-security-is-taxable

(2024). ssa.gov. https://www.ssa.gov/planners/retire/ageincrease.html

(n.d.). schwab.com. https://www.schwab.com/learn/story/social-security-is-taxable-how-to-minimize-taxes

BONUS SECTION: CURRENT-YEAR NUMBERS AND VERIFICATION GUIDE

(n.d.). ssa.gov. https://www.ssa.gov/benefits/retirement/planner/ageincrease.html

(2024-10-10). ssa.gov. https://www.ssa.gov/news/press/releases

(2025-11-14). cms.gov. https://www.cms.gov/newsroom/fact-sheets/2026-medicare-parts-b-premiums-deductibles

(n.d.). medicareinteractive.org. https://www.medicareinteractive.org/understanding-medicare/health-coverage-options/original-medicare-costs/part-b-costs-for-those-with-higher-incomes

(2025-10-10). ssa.gov. https://www.ssa.gov/oact/cola/redlimits.html

(2025). irs.gov. https://www.irs.gov/forms-pubs/about-publication-915

(2024-10-22). irs.gov. https://www.irs.gov/newsroom/irs-releases-tax-inflation-adjustments-for-tax-year-2025

www.ingramcontent.com/pod-product-compliance
Lightning Source LLC
Chambersburg PA
CBHW061220240926
51846CB00006B/1287
9781957515656